JESUS NEVER SAID, "BE CORRECT"

Reflections on Virtues, Vices, and the Commandments

JESUS NEVER SAID, "BE CORRECT"

Reflections on Virtues, Vices, and the Commandments

John W. Currier

JESUS NEVER SAID, "BE CORRECT"
Reflections on Virtues, Vices,
and the Commandments

ISBN 978-1456554132

CONTENTS

THE VIRTUE OF PRUDENCE

THE FOURTH WORD
   "Remember the sabbath day, and keep it holy."

THE FIFTH WORD
   "Honor your father and your mother, . . ."

THE SECOND GREAT COMMANDMENT OF JESUS
   " . . . and your neighbor as yourself."

THE SIXTH WORD
   "You shall not murder."

THE DEADLY SIN OF ANGER

THE SEVENTH WORD
   "You shall not commit adultery."

THE DEADLY SIN OF LUST

THE EIGHTH WORD
   "You shall not steal."

THE DEADLY SIN OF GREED

THE VIRTUE OF TEMPERANCE

THE NINTH WORD
   "You shall not bear false witness . . ."

THE VIRTUE OF JUSTICE

ACKNOWLEDGMENTS

This book began as a series of sermons delivered sporadically between May of 1993 and November of 1994. This book would not exist were it not for the people of Lake Country Congregational Church in Hartland, Wisconsin, with whom I journeyed during that time. Of particular help were the participants in the Tuesday morning Bible class, the Monday morning clergy group and all those who go unnamed simply because of the preacher's tendency to file away words and illustrations that might one day find their way into a sermon. Often such wisdom makes its way into a sermon prefaced by such words as, "Someone once said . . ." or "It's been written that . . ." For those who are not credited by name, I apologize. I'm grateful to the Rev. Karl D. Schimpf for his insights into the theological issues contained in this work, his suggestions made this a better book, and for his mentoring throughout the years. Finally, thanks go to Dr. Lisa Hébert, whose continual support has been meaningful beyond measure.

THE MEAT OF THE SPIRIT

". . . for the letter kills, but the Spirit gives life."
II Corinthians 3:6a

When I was a child and was told, "No," usually by my mother, I often asked "Why?" Frequently, I heard this response: "Because I'm your mother." Today, years later, I know the translation of those words. "Because I'm your mother" or "because I'm your father" really means, "because I'm more experienced than you, more responsible, wiser and recognized by all as qualified to be someone who sets moral boundaries for you."

It was good they offered that moral guidance to me. That is how you raise children in this world. When I reflect on that part of my upbringing, however, I ask what is certainly a perennial question: is the moral character of our society diminishing?

Perhaps, but perhaps not. There are more than enough voices offering their perspective on morals. The Church has been among the most enduring and influential of those voices. But even an institution claiming the authority of God has not been perfect.

The truly powerful and authoritative moral voice is one that speaks to how we should <u>live</u> and not just to how we should <u>believe</u>. The mistake of many church groups has been to focus on belief while losing sight of how to live. The vibrant and colorful tapestry of God's children exists, not so we might make one dimensional declarations about what is right and wrong, or what is acceptable or unacceptable, but so we might know ever deeper and richer layers in our relationships with God and with the Family of God.

In the letter of James we can read these words: "show me your faith without the works, and I will show you my faith by my works." (James 2:18) Earlier in the same letter are these words: "Religion that God our Father accepts as pure and faultless is this: to look after orphans and widows . . ." (James 1:27) If we would have our churches offer a moral voice that might actually be heard, the world must not only hear words <u>about</u> a moral life, but also see concrete expressions <u>in</u> a moral life.

In Paul's first letter to the believers in Corinth, he writes, "I gave you milk to drink, not solid food; (the King James Version says "meat") for you were not able to receive it." (I Cor. 3:2)

This milk and meat contrast offers us a picture of the way a Christian life grows. And yet, at the same time, if not handled carefully, this distinction may present a problem. While the nourishing milk of Biblical basics is important, if a person, growing into maturity, were to drink only milk, they would probably be anemic, in danger of scurvy and certainly not healthy. The same goes with our growing faith.

Spiritual meat is that stuff that makes you chew; the stuff that's sometimes hard to swallow; the stuff that offers what milk cannot offer, and that is the strengthening of our spiritual and moral chewing muscles--muscles that allow us to discern good from evil rather than forcing us to repeat a list of do's and don'ts.

I hope that milk is taken and offers its particular richness. But I hope that meat will be taken, as well, even if it's a little tough. Because chewing on that spiritual meat is truly the only way Christians move beyond uncritical acceptance of belief and onto considered commitment in life. Only then do we make manifest concrete expressions of our faith. There are things to chew on in this Christian life. The Christian experience offers more than a list of correct beliefs to swallow.

Only a year or so after Paul wrote his first letter to the Corinthians, saying that they weren't ready for solid food, he taught them the elementary, and I think meaty, principle: "the letter kills, but the Spirit gives life." (II Cor. 3:6)

Faithfully chewing on some meat of the Spirit, after thankfully drinking the milk of the Letter, can bring us closer to God, closer to our own hearts, and closer together. If we live by the Letter, we can always look for loopholes. But in the Spirit we can find only truth, even if that truth is a truth that sometimes seems silent or elusive, or remains quietly within us. That truth will guide us in the moral life.

The ability to digest some tough meat is going to be important if we hope to grow our spirits and live the moral life. We need to keep chewing.

I have often chewed on the Ten Commandments for

3

moral guidance. The Commandments transcend religious boundaries. The value of the Ten Commandments endures. Along with the Two Great Commandments of Jesus, the Seven Deadly Sins and the Moral Virtues, the Ten Commandments have served well in conversations about the moral life. Herein is a chance to chew on these things.

ABOUT THE COMMANDMENTS

The Ten Commandments are recorded three times in the Bible, twice in Exodus and once in Deuteronomy, with some differences between the lists. Different religious traditions make different use of the Commandments, and that makes discussing them more distracting than we might hope.

The key to understanding the Commandments is found in understanding that the Commandments are not an effort to list legalisms. Additionally, there are no threats here. If we think of the Commandments as rules we obey or break, we miss the point. The Commandments speak of the natural RESPONSE of a community to what God has done.[1] If we begin to think of responding in love to a God who is involved with us, who created us, who sustains life, and who takes life, (that is, who created us mortal) then we will see how commandments help us live. They are not really commandments at all, but rather, thoroughly true statements from God. Literally, they are called "utterances".[2] In the Jewish tradition they are often called the "Ten Words".

THE FIRST WORD

"Then God spoke all these words: I am the Lord your God, who brought you out of the land of Egypt, out of the house of slavery; you shall have no other gods before me."
Exodus 20:1-3

The Jewish tradition says that the first Commandment, is, "I am the Lord your God" and the second is "You shall have no other gods before me." Roman Catholicism combines what Protestants would call the first and second Commandment, saying that the first Commandment is "you shall have no other gods before me and you shall make no graven images." In my tradition, that is, the Protestant Christian understanding, the first Commandment is "You shall have no other gods before me."

Here, I'll use the whole sentence listed at the head of this chapter to serve as the First Commandment.

Sometimes we need to be reminded how to live. For

7

those of us who would call ourselves people of faith, part of that reminder must include placing how we should live, how we *ought* to live, in the context of a relationship with God. With the First Commandment, we have an admirable start.

The First Commandment begins with what God has done. "I am the Lord your God who brought you out of Egypt, out of the land of slavery." It says to us, <u>God has played a part in all that has brought us to this moment</u>: the good and the bad, the joy and the sorrow, the journeys to graduation, the discoveries of love, the losses of loved ones. God has been present in it all.

If we accept that God exists, and that God has been central to our own existence and active in our lives, then the way we live, will reflect that understanding. To make such an acknowledgment, to agree that God exists and has played an ongoing part in our existence, causes us to respond by having no other gods before this God who has been such a part of our lives. To say "Yes" to our relationship with the God of Israel, is to say, by implication, "No" to any other god; be that the god of self, or the god of prosperity or the god of any number of other idolatrous possibilities. If we continue acknowledging that God plays a part in our every breathing moment, the natural response will be that we will have no other gods that might impede the healthy living of our days.

It may help to remember the story of the Ten Commandments. Recall that these words of truth, which would be made manifest in the lives of people, came after they had been led out of slavery in Egypt. God knew the people of Moses belonged somewhere other than in bondage.

Of course, we have our own slaveries. We are often

enslaved to masters who rule our lives in inappropriate ways. If we allow God to lead us out of those slaveries, we gain a marvelous chance to respond to God. In that responsive kind of life we experience one of the deepest meanings of faith. Like the Israelites who were brought out of slavery and led to the place they belonged, we too find that in relationship to God there is a place where we belong, a life we were meant to live.

The first word, the first Commandment, is a Commandment only because it is true and inevitable. If we recognize God as the one who has led us to this moment in our lives, then we can do nothing but accept God as the only God. Then our Creator, God, will be in the center of our lives, the only God to whom we will respond.

The first Commandment is perhaps the most important for this reason: it provides the place upon which we might stand to build lives of integrity. The moral voice of the Church will begin here, when we hear the word, "you shall have no other gods before me" and we respond by saying, "Yes, that is true," then there will be no other gods before the God who has given us life.

With that simple but profound admission, we have a place to stand, a foundation upon which we may begin to build a moral life. It is an important beginning.

THE FIRST GREAT COMMANDMENT OF JESUS

"Just then a lawyer stood up to test Jesus. 'Teacher,' he said, 'what must I do to inherit eternal life?' He said to him, 'What is written in the law? What do you read there?' He answered, 'You shall love the Lord your God with all your heart, and with all your soul, and with all your strength and with all your mind; and your neighbor as yourself.' And he said to him, 'You have given the right answer. Do this, and you will live.'"

Luke 10:25-28

This passage is what people of God are about. This is the sum of what Jesus was trying to teach us. In Matthew's telling of this moment, when Jesus offers what we call the Two Great Commandments, he says, "On these two commandments depend the whole Law and the Prophets." This was his way of saying, "If the Law and the Prophets were given so you'd know how to live as God's creatures, in these two commandments you'll find the essence of being a

11

human as God created humans to be. Here is the distillation of it all."

Jesus wanted us to live well, with some clear understanding of what it meant to live as creatures reflecting the image of our Creator. The greatest reason we stumble through this life is that we lose the clarity we need to live well.

"Love the Lord your God with all your heart and with all your soul and with all your strength and with all your mind." Jesus said, "This is the great and foremost commandment." (Mt.22:38) This is the bedrock of a life lived well. Be clear on that. Start here. This is what we are created for; this and to love one another. This is what we are: humans, created to love God and each other.

Sadly, people have a tendency to lose sight of that truth. We forget who we <u>are</u> and think too much about what we <u>have</u> or what we <u>do</u>. What we are, have and do are tied together, certainly, but if we seek a clear vision of a Godly life, our focus is best aimed at who we <u>are</u>.

Yes, there are things to do. Through the words of Jesus we learn that to follow the two great commandments is what we must do to inherit eternal life. He commanded that we be loving. He taught that what is required for eternal life is love.

But the historical Church and the leaders of that Church have, with all good intentions, obscured the message of Jesus. Or as the Biblical commentator, Ernest Fremont Tittle wrote, "What a complex matter men have made of religion, a matter of ceremonies, rules and all manner of beliefs!"[3] and he goes on to say, "The great concern of religion is not with forms and dogmas and institutions (though these have their place) but with personal relations--man's relation to God and to his fellow man. The great word for these relations is love, as Jesus saw."[4]

Simply put, Jesus taught us to love God and one another, so that we could BE as God intended. Jesus didn't ask for more. He didn't ask for belief or acceptance or conformity. He didn't ask for a theology to be constructed. He didn't ask that an institution be developed. He commanded us to be loving.

The Apostle Paul, and others following Jesus, became Church planters trying to offer an understanding of what we HAVE in the Christian Church--things like salvation and fellowship and hope--and encouraged us to institutionalize in such a way that we might retain those things. That's not all bad, but with that process, the focus changed.

As Christianity grew into predominance in the West, the great defenders of the faith tried to further that teaching by instructing us, in great detail, about what we should DO as Christians. Again, the focus changed.

Because of this great history, what we lose sight of, too easily, is that God loves us, not for what we HAVE, and not for what we DO, but for what we ARE. And, when we're clear on that, we love God, for though we can be grateful for what we have, and though we can seek to be obedient in what we do, we love because we are creatures of a loving Creator who "love because he first loved us."(I John 4:19)

We love God with our hearts, cherishing the relationship, offering thanks. We love God with our souls, taking each breath as an act of worship and praise, understanding how sacred life is. We love God with our strength, knowing that we are made able to do as God calls, because God wills it. We see that our strength is not entirely ours, but God's as well, to be used for God's work. And we love God with our mind, recognizing that religion need not be mindless or unreasonable, but can be informed and rich in truth.

When I was a child we would have Sunday dinner. There was something different about the Sunday Dinner. It was a dining room meal, not a kitchen meal. The preparations were greater. The prayers were more intentional. And maybe the sense was there, a little bit, that one of the courses we indulged in was a common love of God. That love was something we shared.

We all come to each day with our own distinct hungers-- hungers for love, for acceptance, for guidance, for peace, for any number of personal needs. It is in loving God that our hungers are satisfied, directly or indirectly. The love of God is not, however, meant only for our nourishment, but for the nourishment of all of God's children. This love of God is food for the souls of all people, and in loving God we find who we are. The manner in which we should live will become clear if we'll each keep but one thought before us: I love God with my whole being. That must be our first thought, "I love God with my whole being."

ABOUT THE SEVEN DEADLY SINS

The Seven Deadly Sins are not Biblical. At least, they're not listed in the Bible the way the Ten Commandments are. They grew from the considerations of Christians grappling with the idea of the proper Christian life. The Seven Deadly Sins are: envy, pride, greed, gluttony, sloth, lust, and anger.

This list took a while to develop. Originally there were eight deadly sins. One list had pride as the root sin, from which the other seven grew. And depending upon whose list you looked at, you would find "dejection" to be a sin or "melancholy" or "boastfulness". Take your pick. It was the writing of Thomas Aquinas, 1200 years after Jesus, that established, in most minds, what shape the final list would take. And after him, Dante and Chaucer firmed up the cultural place of the Seven Deadly Sins as they are listed above.

These sins are considered deadly because of their ability to generate other sins, and not because they are, in and of themselves, more terrible than other offenses. Still, because of their ability to generate other sin, they have the potential, so say some, of killing the life-giving relationship we have with God, leading the sinner into eternal damnation. And though not all theological perspectives require eternal damnation, the deadly sins are still useful in a discussion of how to live a moral life, because they speak to universal experience as well as to the weight of responsibility that we bear as children of God who have been given free will.

In his book, <u>Whatever Became of Sin?</u>, Karl Menninger laments the fact that we, as a culture, no longer speak of sin, but speak rather, of symptoms.[5] No longer do we speak of attitudes for which we must be responsible, out of which come actions for which we must also be accountable. No, now we speak of conditions to be assessed. Only when we claim responsibility for our attitudes and actions will we be able to be free in the Christian sense.

If we live our lives thinking only of the impact our actions may have on the world, or the consequences our actions may have on us, we will still be bound. That thought process binds us with shackles of self concern, trying to secure our place in the center of the universe rather than being freed to make the world a better place as we act with confidence in relationship with God, who is truly the center of things. Freedom is seen when we can say, "I will act as I ought, because my relationship with God informs me of what I ought to do, and also because I have been taught this since my youth, and the examples of faithful living I see in the lives of those who taught me, from Jesus to my parents, ring true."

You are probably familiar with that moment in the Gospel story when Jesus says to the Jews, ". . . you will know

the truth, and the truth will make you free." (John 8:32)
When you think about it, his words are rather vague. Even
the Jews questioned Jesus about what he meant. The
discussion, as scripture recounts it, was a lengthy one, the
upshot of which is, if you are in a relationship with God that
is honest enough to hear the truths of God, then you will be
free to live as that Divine truth teaches you, no longer
enslaved to sin. That's the freedom Jesus was talking about--
freedom to live, freedom from the shackles of sin.

THE DEADLY SIN OF PRIDE

"Your proud heart has deceived you,
you that live in the clefts of the rock,
whose dwelling is in the heights.
You say in your heart,
"Who will bring me down to the ground?"
Though you soar aloft like the eagle,
though your nest is set among the stars,
from there I will bring you down, says the Lord."
Obadiah 3-4

There are a number of definitions of the word "pride," and before we go too much further, we should understand that while we will speak of the SIN of pride, there are certainly all kinds of pride that are not sinful. The kind of pride we feel when our children do their best, for example, need not be thought of as sinful. Nor is a pride of lions sinful (as a concept), or the best member of a team, who might be called "the pride" of the team. Sinful pride is what

C.S. Lewis called, ". . . the chief cause of misery in every nation and every family since the world began." He said pride ". . . is the complete anti-God state of mind."[6] This is the kind of pride here addressed, and it is deadly.

In a way, as Christians, we are supposed to be proud. I think we can say, without treading too far into dangerous territory, that we Christians should be proud of who and what we are, if we understand who and what we are as related to God and something of which we have no need to be ashamed. But it is a very small step from there to the deadly sin of Pride.

An anonymous book, written in the Middle-Ages, known to us today as The Cloud of Unknowing, gives a hint of how small the step is: "If the thought which comes to you (or which you invite) is full of human conceit regarding your honor, your intelligence, your gifts of grace, your status, talents, or beauty and, if you willingly rest in it with delight, it is the sin of Pride."[7] Simply enjoying a conceited thought is a big enough step to take us to a place of arrogant pride.

In the classical understanding of the sin of Pride, there are three kinds of pride that are dangerous to us. They are the pride of power, the pride of knowledge and the pride of virtue. Or to put it another way, sinful pride can be seen in people who need to be in control, in people who are know-it-alls, and in overly self-righteous people.

Very simply, the worst sorts of idolaters are people who are so blinded by their pride that they cannot see any object of devotion but themselves. These are the people who look not to God, but instead, think that they are, themselves, God. This isn't something that very many people would admit to, thinking themselves God. It seems a ridiculous thing to do. But actions speak louder than words, and if we reflect upon our own actions in this life, they just might reveal to us that we are not so far removed from this kind of sinful pride as we might want to believe.

Those who must be in control reveal a personal belief that they are all-powerful, and not only must they call all the shots in life for themselves and others, they think they are somehow actually up to the task. Know-it-alls believe they are omniscient and cannot be taught anything new by anyone, let alone God. And the self-righteous have forgotten the words of Jesus who said, "No one is good except God alone." (Lk 18:19) The dilemma for the person who is proud becomes, what do you do when you come up against someone who is, in every way, clearly superior? And let me quote C.S. Lewis one more time, for his words are good words: "Unless you know God as [superior] you do not know God at all. As long as you are proud, you cannot know God. A proud man is always looking down on things and people: and, of course, as long as you are looking down, you cannot see something that is above you."[8]

If sin is exploitative in nature, and by that I mean, if sin is behavior in which we engage so that we might gain, so that we might be, to use Biblical language, built up or glorified, then it is pride that stands behind all sin. For God's gain should be our concern, not our own gain.

That makes it doubly important to understand the contrasting idea of humility. For humility is the attitude which allows us to trust in God before we trust in ourselves. What a freedom that could offer us! How liberating it could be to believe so fervently that we trust God with our lives, rather than trust ourselves! As we trust God just a little bit more, remembering that we are creatures of a loving Creator, humility helps us let go, just a little bit, and we begin to live the kind of lives we should live.

The Church can be a very proud institution. A church existing only for the convenience of half-hearted and occasional worshippers is no good, but an active church that has fallen into the sin of pride is to be reviled. The church proud of her buildings and her programs, her music and her perspectives can be sinful, for if WE are the Church, then to be loyal to the Church is to be loyal to ourselves and that's just as prideful and self-idolatrous as if we say "we are God." Hear the words of Obadiah, spoken to a people who were deceived by the pride of their hearts and were living in the giddy heights of pride, only to be told by God that they would be brought down: "Though you soar like the eagle and make your nest among the stars, from there I will bring you down, declares the Lord." (Obadiah 4)

On the other hand, (and after those words we should be glad that there is another hand) the Church existing wherever two or three are gathered together with Christ in their midst, loyal to God alone, can know great humility and can do great things. We have been created in the image of God, glorious creatures, only a little bit lower than angels, as the Psalmist writes of us. (Ps 8:5) We have been given great gifts and great opportunities. But understand this clearly! We have been <u>given</u> great gifts, and great opportunities. We didn't create ourselves or make our own circumstances. We have been <u>given</u> a life, <u>given</u> a place in which we might live it and

22

given a way to live. If we can grab all of that with energy, while at the same time, participating in it with humility, we will be able to do great things . . . for God. We must remember, even as we serve others, if we do anything for someone other than God, ultimately we will find ourselves on the wrong path--a sinfully proud path. All we do, if it is to be worthy of praise at all, is of, for and by God.

THE SECOND WORD

"You shall not make for yourself an idol, whether in the form of anything that is in heaven above, or that is on the earth beneath, or that is in the water under the earth. You shall not bow down to them or worship them; for I the Lord your God am a jealous God, punishing children for the iniquity of parents, to the third and the fourth generation of those who reject me, but showing steadfast love to the thousandth generation of those who love me and keep my commandments."
Exodus 20:4-6

A story is told of a child who, as she was taking her vitamins told her mom that Moses took vitamins too. Her mom asked how she knew this and she said, "God gave him tablets to take down the mountain." As the story goes, the mother explained the true nature of the tablets of the Ten Commandments, while wondering to herself if the Hebrew people found them hard to swallow.

Remember, the precepts offered on Mount Sinai are not, in the Hebrew language, called Commandments, but rather,

Utterances, or the Ten Words of God. As we consider these snippets of Scripture we call Commandments, I urge you to think of them, not as rules, but as statements of fact, or as responses of the Hebrew people to a relationship they had with God.

It's true that the Law of Moses is founded in these words. But these Commandments can be thought of as categories of the law. The laws we read in the book of Leviticus or Deuteronomy fall under these categories. Still, that doesn't make these words rules. It shouldn't surprise us that a people would construct their law upon a small set of agreed upon and commonly understood truths. Continue to think of the Commandments as statements of obvious truth. I think you'll see the value of such an approach.

In our relationship with God, we shall not make idols for ourselves and bow down and worship them. We won't, because as we grow in our relationship with God we'll see that it's not the thing to do.

The temptation, when musing about this Commandment, is to fall into an old cliché and speak of <u>our</u> idols, those things we worship. You know them all, money, possessions, prestige, and so on. You know them. So I won't spend much time on that idea. But do let's take a moment to look behind that process of idolizing something other than God.

Emmet Fox writes that we make a graven image, or idol, whenever we give power to anything <u>but</u> God. We take power, we claim power, we resent power, but those persons and things to which we ascribe power become idols for us.[9] Even if we don't worship them, we are bowing down to them. By allowing others to limit us, be they people, things or circumstances, we give them power over us and, in the process, limit what God can do through us, and, sadly, we begin to see fewer possibilities for glory in the world.

Some people have learned this commandment using the phrase, "graven image." Graven image, then, is an expression we ought to define. As it's written in the book of Exodus, a graven image is an image carved out of either wood or stone. So the Second Commandment tells us that in our relationship with God we will not carve an image of God or any creature, through which we will seek to know power. To us, these days, that seems a primitive thing to do. But we do carve out lives, we talk of carving out an existence, or niches in the working world. We look at what we've carved out in hopes that it will validate us, or give us a place, or give us power, and in that hope, we make an idol. See how subtle the traps are?

We're familiar with the phrase, God is a jealous God. To say such a thing is to say that God must come first, or not at all. Humans who are jealous understand this. We're not speaking of envy here. This is Jealousy, which allows only one center of attention. If we put anything else in center stage, God is removed altogether, not simply shifted to one side. This too, is a statement of fact. If we remove God from the center, God, at least as far as we are concerned, is no longer God. Something else has stepped into that place for us.

I can deal with that part of Jealousy, the recognition that there can be no other. Though I try to avoid conceiving a God who acts in too human a fashion, I can imagine that God wants to be the sole center of our devotional lives. I have no problem imagining that God would simply state the fact that there is only one God; can be only one God. Still, I find the idea troublesome that God will punish children because of the sin of their parents.

The Scriptures say we shall not create for ourselves idols because God is a jealous God punishing even our children if we stray. It's not surprising that people struggle with this idea. We don't want to see God in this vengeful light. And, thankfully, we don't need to. There may indeed be repercussions to our children if we stray from living lives in proper relationship with God, but if there are, we should not put it at God's doorstep, but at our own. Let's at least claim that much responsibility.

Words from Ezekiel help. This is what God said to Ezekiel, ". . . you ask, 'Why does the son not share the guilt of his father?' Since the son has done what is just and right and has been careful to keep all my decrees, he will surely live. The soul who sins is the one who will die. The son will not share the guilt of the father, nor will the father share the guilt of the son. The righteousness of the righteous man will be credited to him, and the wickedness of the wicked will be charged against him." (Ezekiel 18:19-20)   Generational vengeance is not God's way.

What is perhaps, most helpful to remember as we think of this second commandment, is that as God was revealed to Moses and to the people of Israel, God chose to be revealed in a <u>voice</u>, and not in an <u>image</u>. To seek God in an image, rather than through a word, is inappropriate. To make an image, to which we might bow down and worship, be that figuratively or literally, sets up a rival to God's revelation and

28

can lead us to the place where we wrongly think we can call upon the power of the image. And the Second Commandment knows this. Remember how it reads. It says that in our healthy relationships with God we will not make idols, FOR OURSELVES. Images are always made <u>for us</u>, for our purposes. God asks only that we be open to the word of truth which might be revealed to us.

In reality, this commandment is about creating God in our image. This is about relegating God to a lesser place, a place that can be shut off and ignored, a place that is limited and confined by what we know and by what we desire, a process that implies we have power over God--a process that starts us down the road to being idols ourselves.

If we are going to make this commandment useful, we need to see the truth of it in our lives. Think about what has power over you -- what you adore and what you fear -- your boss, your spouse, your schedule, your list of things that must be done or acquired. People often make the mistake of thinking that something possessed or achieved will somehow make them more worthwhile. Some people honestly can't imagine that they, themselves, are worthwhile creatures simply because God created them and loves them. But we are worthwhile, simply because God created us worthy of love. The only worth that matters comes from God. If that rings true with you, then you're well on the way to living a life of praise. You can still know achievement in this life, but in the kind of relationship with God we're considering, achievements become expressions of gratitude for the gifts God has given to you; achievements become acts of praise to the God who loves you for who you are, not for what you do.

The scale of worth is too easily skewed in our world. Adjust your scale. Idols have no true power or worth. But idols we make for ourselves have a way of turning on us and taking power over us, even if it's a false power they exert. In a healthy and growing relationship with God, you shall not create idols for yourselves, for God, who loves us for who we are, will be enough. It's that simple.

THE DEADLY SIN OF GLUTTONY

"Those who keep the law are wise children, but companions of gluttons shame their parents."
Proverbs 28:7

"To what then will I compare the people of this generation, and what are they like? They are like children sitting in the marketplace and calling to one another, 'We played the flute for you, and you did not dance; we wailed, and you did not weep.' For John the Baptist has come eating no bread and drinking no wine, and you say, 'He has a demon', the Son of Man has come eating and drinking, and you say, 'Look, a glutton and a drunkard, a friend of tax collectors and sinners!' Nevertheless, wisdom is vindicated by all her children."
Luke 7:31-35

I must confess that of the deadly sins, this one makes me the most uncomfortable. I love to eat and I'm very good at it. That talent, however, makes my risk of appearing the hypocrite especially grave.

31

The popular understanding of gluttony relates to over-eating. But it can apply to other areas of our lives. We speak of being a glutton for work or punishment. An eager reader of books might be called a glutton for words. There is, I've learned, an animal called the "glutton". It is a voracious animal in the weasel family.

Let me use the most familiar understanding, that of over-eating, to throw some light on other kinds of gluttony, for they are all related.

Allow me, as well, to avoid the cliché, or at least let me get it out of the way in a hurry, by saying, we all know how fortunate we are, how abundant food and other consumable items are in our land, while others in our world go without. We all know that. Many of the most fortunate among us have felt a little guilt about it at one time or another. Abundance and need are truths we live with and deal with through such avenues as volunteer work and charitable giving. The words of Jesus: "from everyone who has been given much shall much be required"(Luke 12:48) speak of a responsibility that most people willingly accept, whether our wealth is found in dollars, family, friends or faith.

But how we deal with gluttony in our own hearts speaks of something other than a sense of social responsibility or love of humanity. It speaks of the character of our relationship with God and of the gifts with which God has blessed us.

Gluttons don't dine, they eat. Gluttons don't savor, they devour. Still, this is only a symptom of a deeper condition which points to why gluttony is a sin at all.

Gluttony is a sin for a number of reasons. First, it is a sin because it abuses something that is essential. God has created us with a need to eat, and has created a world with food. (This is, by the way, something like another deadly sin: Lust. To survive we must procreate, but some people abuse the gift of sexuality. More on that in a later chapter.) To survive we must eat. To over-eat, however, does not mean we will survive better. To over-eat is to be, very simply, wasteful. And in a world of want, were I to construct my own list of sins, wastefulness would be near the top.

Second, Gluttony is a sin because the focus on food makes us indifferent to the glory of God's gifts and God's Creation. When we focus only on stuffing our face, our attention is diverted away from the gift of God's provision, on to the task of consuming. That shows ingratitude.

Third, Gluttony is a sin because it is a solitary pursuit. It focuses on the individual and thinks only of satisfying the appetite. A meal should be for nourishment so that we might go on in our days fulfilling the work to which God has called us. But a glutton eats to be selfish. Gluttons, even in fine company, rarely share anything with anyone.

In summary, Gluttony is sinful because it is wasteful, ungrateful and selfish. And by the way, this sounds very much like the dieter who only focuses on food, hearing the food commercials so loudly, frequenting the refrigerator to see what's there, counting all sorts of nutritional numbers checking all sorts of caloric and fat gram scales and tables, to focus on an ungrateful, solitary and, often, wasteful pursuit.

So you see, Gluttony really is not just about over-eating. It's about over-concern for oneself. The scripture readings show us that gluttony has long been considered disgusting.

Such may have been the case out of jealousy. It might have been that only those in the upper class had the opportunity to be gluttonous. Still, we see in the words of scripture that to be seen as a glutton is not a good thing. "The Son of Man has come eating and drinking; and you say, 'Behold, a glutton, and a drunkard. . .'"

What makes Gluttony deadly is that it cuts us off from relationships with God and others, by focusing only on our relationship with food. Us and food. God is removed from the picture and so are others. And this sin is deadly in another way. Unlike most of the other deadly sins, gluttony can have real and dangerous physical consequences. It can be truly deadly.

We Americans are not known for our healthy eating habits. Fast food is evidence that we want to get some food in us. I doubt it is an expression of the desire to appreciate what God has given to us. I went to the internet site, Amazon.com and typed in the subject "religion" to see what would come up. There were 18,416 nonfiction book titles. Under the heading "cooking" there were 25,776.[10] We could probably assume, then, that we think about food considerably more often than we think of religion, and I doubt many would argue the point.

Remember this Beatitude that Jesus spoke to us: "Blessed are those who hunger and thirst for righteousness, for they will be filled." (Matthew 5:6) That is the hunger we should focus upon. For in righteousness we learn moderation. In righteousness we remember the story of God providing Manna in the wilderness for the people of Moses. And we're told, ". . . those who gathered much had no over, and those who gathered little had no shortage; they gathered as much as each of them needed." (Exodus 16:18)

So how are we to deal with gluttony, we who have the means to have a great feast on most any day? It's important to ask: What's our motive? To feast in celebration for God's gifts is an appropriate thing to do. To eat until the button on our pants pops is not so appropriate. Gluttony is not the same as feasting. The first definition of "Feast" in the dictionary is "joyful religious anniversary," and the further defining characteristics of a feast, while including sumptuous meals, also includes celebration of something other than our own appetites, and the inclusion of guests, sharing in fellowship.[11]

The real and constant dilemma of the Christian is to seek perfection where perfection cannot be attained. But if we do anything less than seek perfection; if we say, "we know we can never be perfect so we'll just settle for what we are," then we deny ourselves the chance to move toward perfection. It was Jesus who said, "Be perfect, therefore, as your heavenly Father is perfect." (Matthew 5:48) Which is not to say that we are to become God-like in our perfection, but that we are to become fully human; to become what we were created to be. As God is perfectly God, we are to be perfectly God's children, whole and complete, marked by integrity and devotion to God, not by devotion to food or any other idol.

How we move on to that kind of wholeness is something with which all Christians struggle. It appears, though, that part of what we were created to be pulls us (kicking and screaming most of the time) toward a place where we will see everything in a spiritual perspective.

35

Eating is spiritual. One important mechanism that might help to communicate this idea is one familiar to us all, but maybe not as common as it should be. That mechanism is saying prayers of thanks at our meals. And by the way, I don't think all prayers must be vocalized, if we are truly conscious of our efforts to pray. You might be familiar with this prayer. "Good bread, good meat, Good Lord, let's eat!" My goodness! That opens the door to gluttony in the worst way. We can do better.

Usually, when I pray at a meal, whether silent or vocalized, it's either something made up at the moment, something passing and generally forgetful, or something memorized from my childhood that is so familiar that I don't really pay attention to it. And so I've decided to write a prayer for a particular purpose: to help return the focus of my spirit and my life to its proper place. I want to share it with you, and if you can use it, feel free. Verse tends to be easier to remember, so I've written it that way. It goes like this:

> We, who are so blessed and free,
> Dear God, our needs are very few.
> Let our deepest hunger be
> To do what you would have us do.
> As, with Thanks, we feast today,
> Feed our Spirits, this we pray.

> Amen.

THE THIRD WORD

"You shall not make wrongful use of the name of the Lord your God, for the Lord will not acquit anyone who misuses his name."
Exodus 20:7

The Ten Commandments, these utterances or statements of fact that become manifest in our lives as we build our respective relationships with God, have a way of causing us to ask questions.

The two obvious questions that this third commandment raises are, what is the Lord's name? and, what does it mean to misuse it, or as the more familiar version puts it, to take this name "in vain"? Let's consider some answers to those questions, answers that might have applied to the ancient Hebrew people, and those that might apply to us in our day. Also, let's add what may be a more valuable question: "Do we really, honestly, think that God's name has power?" And let's acknowledge, right away, that the honest reply to that question is, "Yes, we do" and "No, we don't."

In Scripture, the name of the Lord that Moses received is an unpronounceable bunch of Hebrew consonants, to which we have added vowels so that we could pronounce it as, "Yahweh". The early Hebrews wouldn't pronounce it, not only because it was unpronounceable, but because they considered it a name not to be profaned by mere human tongues. When Moses stood before the burning bush, he said to God, When I say God has sent me and the Israelites ask me what your name is, "What shall I say to them?" the response of God, was, "I am who I am. Thus you shall say to the Israelites, 'I AM has sent me to you.'"(Exodus 3:13-14) This name, "I AM", comes from that strange bunch of Hebrew consonants and is linguistically related, somehow, to the verb "to be". It could mean "I am he who is" or "I will be who I will be" or "He causes to be". And it may mean little more than "I am un-named." I am who I am.

Whatever the case, the ancient Hebrew people didn't want to misuse the Divine name because they respected it and also because they shared a belief that to know the name of a person was to have power over that person. As one commentator puts it, "To speak the name is to involve the person."[12] And it followed for those people that to call upon God's name was to call upon God's power. You need only think of the words of Scripture to see it's true. Phrases like this abound: "Call on the name of the Lord," "Prophesy in the name of the Lord," "Blessed be the name of the Lord," and so on. They thought the name, Yahweh, was powerful.

So we should ask, what does it mean to take this name in vain? To take the name in vain, can probably best be translated as to take the name "for nothing" or "for emptiness."[13]   The Hebrews saw the power of Yahweh and believed in it.   For them, to misuse the name, to take it as something frivolous or meaningless or powerless, was wrong.

For us today, the name we give to our Creator most usually is, not Yahweh, but "God," and I think Emmet Fox speaks a deeper truth when he writes that "The real name of God for you is your idea of God . . ."[14]   He makes a very interesting contribution to our consideration of these commandments as Ten Words of God, or ten statements of fact in adding, "Moses says here, you cannot take the name of the Lord, thy God in vain.   You cannot do it."[15]   That's the truth of this commandment!   You very well might be able to use the name of the Lord your God in a curse.   But it will not be in vain.   Remember the Commandment--all of it.   "You shall not make wrongful use of the name of the Lord your God, for the Lord will not acquit anyone who misuses his name."   Which is to say, you cannot take the name of God for nothing, because it is not nothing, and the name you use, the idea of God that informs your way of living, will bring what consequences it will.   But know that there will be consequences.

That may sound foreboding, but hear Emmet Fox again. He says that the question "do you believe in God?" is not an especially important one.   He says, "the only intelligent question is what kind of God do you believe in, because everybody believes in some God, even those who do not like the word.   And you cannot believe in any kind of God without getting the result of that."   He goes on to say that whatever your idea of God is will affect your life in every way.   If your idea of God is a good and loving God, then the

results of that will show in your life. If you believe in a harsh and judgmental God, then your life will show that too. If your idea of God is one that leads you to say, "'God sent this trouble into my life for a good purpose, and I must put up with it.'. . . [then] you will put up with it. You will not overcome it." It's the thought that counts. It is your idea of God that truly names God for you. And whatever the name, it cannot mean nothing.[16]

Now let's ask the third question that was mentioned earlier. Do we truly think that the name of God has power? And remember the answer? "Yes, we do," and "No, we don't."

We do misuse the name of God. In the most cynical way, we see manipulators calling upon the name of God to legitimize personal agendas, be they political or religious or even financial, seeking worldly gain rather than spiritual transformation.

The ancient Hebrews understood that there were people out there who would misuse the name of God for personal gain, calling upon the power of the name, assuming it could be used without there being a personal price to pay. But remember, those who would manipulate cannot use the name of the Lord in vain, for, as we've said, whenever one uses the name of God, there will be consequences. I cringe when I watch political figures catering to religious groups to gain a vote. The name of God is not being used in vain, but it is being misused. I also wonder, what kind of price is being paid?

So, yes, we do think the name has power. We use it, and misuse it, sometimes for personal gain, and sometimes in an honest effort to glorify God. We warn our friends to be careful about what they ask for in their prayers. Something in us tells us not to call upon God's name without expecting some result--even if we're only being superstitious. We do think there is power in the name. And yet, we also think the name has no power. Bear with me and you'll see what I mean.

The most popular understanding of this commandment has to do with swearing or profanity. The Hebrew understanding included the idea that one ought not swear by the name of the Lord. But that means we're not to say, "I swear to God I'll do this or that." Jesus pointed that out rather clearly, "Let your word be 'Yes, Yes' or 'No, No'; anything more than this comes from the evil one." (Mt. 5:37) But when WE think of swearing we usually think less of pledges and more of profanity or angry curses.

When the Hebrews were angry they might ask God to damn someone. But if they did, and I imagine it was a rare occurrence, they meant just what they said. They didn't mean, "heck". They meant "I want God to damn you, to condemn you." Powerful stuff. They didn't take the name of the Lord for emptiness.

When we mutter or yell out a profanity that includes God's name in it, we make the mistake of thinking that there's power added to our angry expressions when God's name is included. But the real profanity is not in the use of religious language to add emphasis to our curse, but in using God's name in a way that assumes that God's name has no real power. It's taking the name of the Lord, for emptiness. Because we don't want to express more than our anger. We certainly don't want God to damn others. At least not usually. And it's a mistake to think we can use the name of God so flippantly, because, once again, it cannot be done. Interestingly enough, the person who employs God's name in curses most often, usually expects little if any involvement of God in their worldly affairs. Those less inclined to use profanity, more typically believe that God is involved in their lives. It shows.

We all know that religious language fills only a small corner of the word category named, "profanity." It's striking how widespread profanity is. Profanity includes references to our sexuality and to our bodily functions; both, incidentally, gifts from God. Very few of us can claim that a profanity has never escaped our lips. When those attributes of our mortal selves rear their ugly heads, we can be quietly grateful for forgiveness.

When we call ourselves "creatures", we are, implicitly, taking on the name of the Lord our God, our Creator, the One who is and Who allows us to be. If we take that name in vain, for nothing, the people who look at us will see hypocrites, and they'll hear hypocrisy in our language. But if we take the name seriously, our seriousness will show in our lives, for we will live with new power. By our example, that power will work in the lives of our children and in the life of the world as well.

We shall not use the Lord our God's name in vain because we cannot. To use the Lord's name means that there will be consequences. Period. Hopefully, our understanding of God, built in relationship with God, will steer us to using God's name in a way that leads to glorious consequences.

The first commandment taught us that there is no other God but our Creator God, who is revealed in a voice and by a word of truth. And that understanding has shown us that we will make no idols to which we will bow down, for "God is spirit and those who worship him must worship in spirit and truth". (John 4:24) And a God such as that, is a God whose name will not be used in vain, no matter how hard we try.

THE DEADLY SIN OF SLOTH

"Even though we speak in this way, beloved, we are confident of better things in your case, things that belong to salvation. For God is not unjust; he will not overlook your work and the love that you showed for his sake in serving the saints, as you still do. And we want each one of you to show the same diligence so as to realize the full assurance of hope to the very end, so that you may not become sluggish, but imitators of those who through faith and patience inherit the promises."
Hebrews 6:9-12

I worked as a civil servant for a time. In the building where I worked, there was a bulletin board--the kind of bulletin board that exists in all such places: the promotions opportunities board. People would drift by and glance at the board, and if something was seen that might offer a higher pay grade in their area of expertise, they would linger a while. One day I saw a merit promotion announcement--an amendment to a previous announcement about an opening for a personnel clerk. The amendment was to delete the following:

"4) PERSONAL CHARACTERISTICS

    A. EXHIBITS A FRIENDLY HELPFUL ATTITUDE TOWARD THE PUBLIC AND FELLOW EMPLOYEES IN THE PERFORMANCE OF DUTIES.

    B. EXHIBITS A DEDICATION TO PERFORMING WORK OF HIGH STANDARD."

I couldn't believe my eyes. Apparently they couldn't get someone who could be helpful and friendly, dedicated to a high standard of work, so they deleted those requirements!

The example serves to show just how critical it is to be aware of the deadly sin of sloth, and by sloth I mean: laziness, idleness, sluggardlyness.

Sloth is not seen in someone who is at thankful rest, but rather in the one who is not invested in life and is just letting things run their course. In other words, the slothful person is simply getting through life.[17]

The real work of faith is not getting through life, but getting life right. The real work is in building a healthy and life giving relationship with God. If we find ourselves in a "getting through life" attitude toward our relationship with God, we might also find that we are more concerned about ourselves than with our relationship with God. We may find we are no longer making time for prayer. We might discover we're just going through the motions, indifferent to the sufferings of others or, worst of all, lacking in joy for this great life God has presented to us as a gift of overflowing love. We may hear ourselves saying things like, "I'm a good person" or "It works for me." And such signs of self-concern indicate a slothful faith.

There are lazy people in all walks of life and in all brands of religion. But sloth is deadly in any relationship we have, not only in the relationship we have with God. If we don't invest faithfully and diligently in our marriages, there comes a time when the only possible relationship is one that is on the surface--one that exists only for "me", and not for "us". There might be a marriage that other people see, but the love and trust that brought about an initial commitment can fade into a slothful and self-serving "getting through life" routine that kills the relationship.

If we're lucky, sloth will not blind us to the sad state of affairs we've entered into. If we see we're just getting through, we'll be able to start bridging the gap between getting through life and truly living life.

Bridging that gap is characterized by this: the anticipation that something is about to happen. Something is about to happen, now, every moment. When we pray we must pray with anticipation. When we worship, we must come with anticipation. When we greet each day, we must greet it with anticipation. We must not just go through the motions. Because it is in anticipation that we open ourselves to the wisdom and power of God. It is in anticipation that we reach a bit higher toward the one we love. In anticipation we gain a willingness to act as God directs.

Once a friend of mine said, "You know, Mother Teresa could have gone anywhere in the world and lived a life of honor and comfort. But she continued to stay in Calcutta. And I can't imagine she ever got up in the morning and said,

"Oh no, another rotten day in Calcutta!" She woke up with anticipation that God was at work."[18]

It's anticipation in love that keeps us on the path that lifts our spirits, and it is anticipation that encourages us always to aspire to higher and higher things. That anticipation, as we wait upon the God we love, is what keeps us from the deadly sin of Sloth.

There is a verse, author unknown, that applies:

There are two kinds of people on earth today;
Just two kinds of people, no more to say.
Not the good and the bad, for 'tis well understood
That the good are half bad and the bad are half good.
No, the two types of people on earth I mean
Are the people who lift and the people who lean.

May we always be the people who lift!

A PRIMER ON THE CLASSICAL VIRTUES

St. Thomas Aquinas begins the second part of his great work, The Summa Theologica, with a discussion about human habits. The good habits he calls "virtues", something we'd all like to have. Then Aquinas breaks his list down into three groups.

The three kinds of virtues--the three kinds of good habits are: Intellectual, Moral and Theological.

The **Intellectual** Virtues are Wisdom, Science and Understanding. These are the kind of virtues that schools should teach. We're not going to consider them here.

The **Theological** Virtues are familiar to us. They are: Faith, Hope and Love. The Church talks about those on a fairly regular basis, so we'll set those aside for now.

It is the **Moral** Virtues we'll deal with, because they speak of how we should live. The Moral Virtues direct all other aspects of a life well-lived, directing even the other kinds of virtues. Let me list the Moral Virtues. They are Prudence, Fortitude, Temperance and Justice. They're also called the

Cardinal Virtues because they play a particularly important part in the reasoned life. The word "Cardinal" means "primary" and, in its Latin origins, is related to a word meaning "hinge". A moral life swings primarily on the hinge of the Cardinal Virtues. A more fitting designation might be "Pivotal" Virtues.[19]

THE VIRTUE OF PRUDENCE

"For which of you, intending to build a tower, does not first sit down and estimate the cost, to see whether he has enough to complete it?"
Luke 14:28

The first of the Four Cardinal Virtues is Prudence. It is first because, in the words of Thomas Aquinas, "Prudence is the principle of all the virtues absolutely."[20] It is meant to be the guiding virtue in all of life.

We typically think of someone who is prudent as being cautious or even prudish. But the word "prudence" means something rather different. It means, very simply, "Common Sense".[21] If only we had more common sense, more practical wisdom in the world. Common Sense doesn't seem so common these days. There are adequate amounts of cunning and sufficient plotting, but very little prudence.

Sometimes we Christians think we're supposed to be more concerned with being good and doing good than with having common sense. Jesus wasn't so narrow in his thinking. Jesus sent his disciples out with these words, "See, I am sending you out like sheep into the midst of wolves; so be wise as serpents, and innocent as doves." (Matthew 10:16) as if to say, don't forget to acknowledge the practical realities of life in this world.

Jesus encouraged us to be prudent, and did it in a way that spoke of the fullness of the meaning of the word. In asking which of us undertakes a project without doing some calculations first, he was saying, do two things in your decision-making life, whether your decisions are to follow me, or to do something else altogether:

Think your decision through.

Consider the consequences.

Christians who struggle with moral dilemmas know better than most people that sometimes there simply isn't a desirable course of action. There truly are times when choosing between the lesser of two evils is the best we can do. That's when prudence, or common sense, becomes most valuable.

In the English countryside are very narrow lanes. They're two lane roads that are about one-and-a-half car-widths wide. The only shoulder is a hedge that is about eight feet high, which doesn't allow you to see anything except the road. They're winding roads and, because of the hedges, you can't see around the corners.

Thomas Hobbes made use of these hedges in a wonderful analogy of the life of faith. He suggested that the hedges serve, not as impediments to us, but rather as a means of keeping us on the road. But he also said that the hedges don't force us to stay on the road. We can go through the hedge and strike out on our own. If we do, however, especially if we have no map, or if we're unfamiliar with the territory beyond the hedge, we do so at our own risk.[22]

Let's say that the hedges represent religion. Prudence, will tell us that religion is a good thing; keeping us on a road toward our destination of God. The facts may tell us that moving beyond the hedge is allowable, even though prudence will say it's risky. In addition, prudence will tell us that we should count the cost before we leave the road. It is the theological version of "Look before you leap". But this is not just an encouragement to be cautious--not only an exhortation to take the safe path. Prudence serves to acknowledge risk so we might make difficult decisions with care.

Some might say that Jesus broke through the hedge, blazing new trails for the religion of his day. Maybe Martin Luther did, making a new way for the Protestant Reformation. Perhaps even the Pilgrims did, seeking a new, freer way of worship. Perhaps others have, and perhaps you will, one day. But if you make a decision to break through some hedge somewhere, remember to be prudent. If prudence is at work as we make tough decisions, we'll be well on the way to living good and moral lives.

Think things through and count the cost. That's common sense.

THE FOURTH WORD

"Remember the Sabbath Day, and keep it holy."

Exodus 20:8

There are two versions of this fourth utterance of God in the Bible. After the commandment itself, the Exodus version reads: "Six days you shall labor and do all your work. But the seventh day is a sabbath to the Lord your God . . . For in six days the Lord made the heavens and earth, the sea, and all that is in them, but rested the seventh day. . ." (Exodus 20:9-11)

Then in Deuteronomy, we read: "Remember that you were a slave in the land of Egypt . . . therefore the Lord your God commanded you to keep the sabbath day."(Deut. 5:15)

Which is it? Are we to keep the Sabbath holy so we might reflect God's creativity by modeling six days of creation and then resting on the seventh? Or are we to keep the Sabbath holy so we'll remember the great things God has done in our lives?   Are we to honor the work of God in and through the Exodus by working for six days, reminiscent of the time in bondage, and then resting on the seventh to bring to mind the liberation from slavery? If you remember the Exodus story, you'll know that it was more complicated than that. Though slavery of the Hebrews stopped at the Exodus, wandering and warring followed before they came to the rest of the Promised land. A better plan might be to work for five days, wander around and make war on your neighbors for the 6th day and then rest on the seventh.

The truth is, these two versions of this commandment sought to make the Sabbath a part of ordinary existence, a part of everyday life so that all could partake, even the slaves--even the alien residents.(Exodus 20:10b) The Sabbath is not bound up with restrictions of place or sacrifice, it's not a particular festival, it's part of everyone's day, so that all people can rest.

Jesus was called to task, one Sabbath day, when his disciples picked grain because they were hungry. This moment emphasizes both the negative and positive aspects of the Sabbath. On the negative side we hear the Pharisees saying, "You shall not do any work." When they witnessed this work, they didn't see anything but the negative. They said, and I paraphrase, "What your disciples are doing is against the law!"

There is a positive side to the commandment as well. After telling us what we won't do, the commandment tells us what we will do. "You shall remember that you were a slave and the Lord God brought you out of Egypt." You shall remember the Exodus. Or, from the other version of the commandment, the understanding that "you shall remember that after the work of creation, God rested on the seventh day."

This is not a command to honor a particular day, as much as it is, an encouragement to understand the Sabbath as more than simple rest. To keep the Sabbath holy is to participate in the universe as God created it. The Sabbath has a part in every moment. God created the universe with a Sabbath, a refuge from work and worry, a time and a place of peace. The Sabbath is part of the fabric of creation--not something we make or mark, but something we REMEMBER.

Do you see? The positive side in this commandment is the message of liberation and rest. And Jesus drives this point home in a way that might be helpful to us. We don't need to get hung up on which day of the week is the Sabbath. In saying, "The Son of Man is the Lord of the Sabbath," Jesus is saying, "Look to me for your liberation and your rest." We read of Jesus saying, "The truth will set you free," and "Come to me all who are weary and heavy laden and I will give you rest." The point of the Sabbath is not so much the calendar, as it is the focus on remembering what God has done, sharing in the liberating message of the Christ and taking the opportunity we've been given to rest in the midst of an often too busy world.

Having said that, however, let's acknowledge, as well, that the Sabbath as a day on the calendar is indeed important.

Emerson wrote, "The Sunday is the core of our civilization, dedicated to thought and reverence."[23] My goodness, if Sunday is still the core of our civilization, to what is it dedicated now? Yard care? Sports? Shopping?

Remember the Sabbath and keep it holy? Not these days. Remember when everything was closed on Sundays? No more.

The Sabbath, as a day set aside, is drifting further and further from our experience, and such a day will not come back into our experience if the Church DECREES it. It will become a part of our lives only if we DECIDE it.

In a wonderful novel by Robert Raynolds, entitled, The Sinner of Saint Ambrose, the main character says, "I went to church frequently now and resumed a practice I had dropped some years ago, of rising early to add an hour to my day in which I could read and meditate . . . This would pass in our society for being quite religious. But to my way of thinking, being religious is not a matter of acting this way or that an hour here and there in the day. . . . I would rather say that a religious man is one who keeps *a constant appointment with God.*"[24](emphasis mine)

I'm becoming more convinced of the value of remembering the Sabbath. Not so we might be restricted by it, but so that we might be liberated by it, freed from a world that would gladly bleed every drop of life from us to further passing causes; freed from the idea that we must always be in servitude; freed so we might simply rest from time to time and know that God loves us.

Maybe this is where this commandment shows its inevitability. If we remember the Sabbath, it will be kept Holy.

Jesus taught us that the Sabbath is not ruled by days, but by the relationships we each have with God. Keeping a constant appointment with God reminds us of how free we can be, and as we remember the Sabbath and keep it holy, we truly know the blessing of rest.

THE FIFTH WORD

"Honor your father and your mother, so that your days may be long in the land that the Lord your God is giving you."
Exodus 20:12

When you look at the order of the commandments, you see that this commandment stands as something of a bridge between commandments that have to do more directly with our relationships with God, and commandments that deal most pointedly with our relationships among people. In the middle of the commandments is this commandment, the only one that offers a promise. "Honor your father and your mother, so that your days may be long in the land the Lord your God is giving you." Both God and people are included.

"Honor your father and your mother." Brevard Childs fills out the Biblical understanding of the verb "to honor" as he writes, "To honor is to prize highly (Prov. 4:8), to show respect, to glorify and exalt. Moreover, it has nuances of caring for and showing affection (Ps. 91:15). It is a term frequently used to describe the proper response to God and

59

is akin to worship (Ps. 86:9)."[25] How many of us honor our parents to that extent?

Let's look at this Commandment in two ways. First, in a more abstract and theoretical way, and second, in a more practical way. The theoretical says that parents ought to be honored simply because they are parents, and not because of their achievements or because of emotions, or because such honor serves society, but because parents are parents. We all know that there are parents in the world who deserve no honor, but that's the practical part. Stick with me for just a moment and you'll see where I'm going.

B. Davie Napier suggests that parents are to be honored because it is through parents that life enters the world. Napier puts words into God's mouth to make the point. He has God saying: "Your life is my gift. I created you in the image of the divine; the essential breath of life is transmitted through your parents. . . The life your parents bear and give to you is my life. To dishonor them is to dishonor me!"[26]

We know, of course, that "the land that the Lord your God is giving" was originally understood as the Promised Land waiting for the people of Moses. But we could say that the land God gives to us, in which we hope to live long, is, at least metaphorically, the land of life. To live long in this land is more than a statement of time, but also "points to the rich blessing of the society which is in harmony with the divine order."[27] And that Divine order includes honoring the life givers.

There's an old story of the child who was asked, on Mother's Day, what the Sunday school lesson was for the day. To which the child responded, "It was a commandment:

Humor your father and your mother." I would hope that honoring our parents would go further than humoring them, but sometimes that is about as far as it goes, which brings us to the practical part of this.

Joy Davidman wrote that the "crude and naked" meaning of this commandment is ". . . a society that destroys the family destroys itself."[28] And she recalls one of the fairy tales of the Brother's Grimm. It makes a wonderful point. It's very short and worth consideration.

THE OLD GRANDFATHER'S CORNER

Once upon a time there was a very old man who lived with his son and daughter-in-law. His eyes were dim, his knees tottered under him when he walked, and he was very deaf. As he sat at table, his hand shook so that he would often spill the soup over the table-cloth, or on his clothes, and sometimes even he could not keep it in his mouth when it got there. His son and daughter were so annoyed to see his conduct at the table that at last they placed a chair for him in a corner behind the screen, and gave him his meals in an earthenware basin quite away from the rest. He would often look sorrowfully at the table with tears in his eyes, but he did not complain.

One day, thinking sadly of the past, the earthenware basin, which he could scarcely hold in his trembling hands, fell to the ground and was broken. The young wife scolded him well for being so careless, but he did not reply, only sighed deeply. Then the daughter bought him a wooden bowl for a penny, and gave him his meals in it.

Some days afterwards the son and daughter saw their little

boy, who was about four years old, sitting on the ground and trying to fasten together some pieces of wood.

"What are you making, my boy?" asked his father.

"I'm making a little bowl for papa and momma to eat their food in when I grow up," he replied.

The husband and wife looked at each other without speaking for some minutes. At last they began to shed tears, and went and brought their old father back to the table, and from that day he always took his meals with them, and was never again treated unkindly.[29]

Many of us remember a time when elders were respected for their wisdom and their experience. Much of that respect, unfortunately, is gone. While there was a time when what parents knew was useful to the livelihood of their children, now, with lifestyles changing, new technologies driving the culture, different business models directing our work and incredibly busy schedules eating up our time, less of what elders could teach seems useful to the young. That's especially sad. Additionally, as we confess the existence of those who would neglect or abuse children, we can legitimately ask, how can we honor all our mothers and fathers?

Here is the Christian response: It is a two-fold response. First of all, if we are in a growing relationship with God, the giver of life, we will honor our mother and father as the commandment, this utterance of God, states. It will become a part of our character. But in order to achieve that, we might well have to ask, as did Jesus, "Who is my mother, and who are my brothers?" The answer is, our mother and brothers (and fathers) are those who <u>truly</u> give us life, those who <u>truly</u> nurture us, those who <u>truly</u> raise us up to responsible maturity, those we naturally honor.

So the responsibility for this lies both with parents, who must do what is deserving of honor, and with children, who must see beyond the incredibly strong ties of biology to the even stronger ties of the Spirit. For through spiritual ties we will know our mothers and our fathers most richly, and then they will be truly honored.

THE SECOND GREAT COMMANDMENT OF JESUS

"You shall not hate in your heart anyone of your kin; you shall reprove your neighbor, or you will incur guilt yourself. You shall not take vengeance or bear a grudge against any of your people, but you shall love your neighbor as yourself: I am the Lord."
Leviticus 19:17-18

This is the second great commandment. The first was "You shall love the Lord your God with all your heart with all your soul, with all your strength and with all your mind." Jesus said of these two commandments, that they were the basis of the "Law and the Prophets"(Matthew 22:40). As was said earlier, if you were to distill the message of the scriptures he knew, which means, basically, the Old Testament as Christians know it, it would come down to this: Love God and your neighbor as yourself. That is the essence of the Law and the Prophets and the message of Jesus.

65

"Love your neighbor as yourself", is a command. This is an <u>order</u>, not a statement of truth to be evidenced in our relationship with God, as we've suggested in regard to the Ten Commandments. This is an order, at least as the Gospel writers, Matthew and Mark relate it. If we want to know eternal life, we must hear the command and obey it: love God and, more to the point of this chapter, our neighbor as ourselves. That's what it takes.

This commandment to love our neighbor as ourselves is so familiar to us that sometimes, like all that is overly familiar, it gets taken for granted and loses its power. We <u>know</u> that we are to love our neighbors. And we <u>know</u> that we are to love ourselves. That's the obvious part. And we probably understand why we should love our neighbor as ourselves. We know that in such an act of love, we reflect more clearly the image of God that was created in us. God's love becomes more evident as we love one another.

There are, however, some less obvious considerations. The version from Leviticus that heads this chapter speaks to some of them. As we love our neighbor, we are to be concerned about them. This is not simply affection or sentimentality. This is love. There are, in the Greek of the New Testament, four different words for love, four kinds of love, ranging from the love we carry for our friends to the love we hold for nations or for spouses as well as to that love called, "Agapé". That is the word Jesus used when he said, "Love your neighbor as yourself." Agapé. And that kind of love is concerned about the character of the other, the safety of the other, agapé will rebuke another, if that is called for, and agapé is a love that forgives. It is the same love that allowed Jesus to say of his executioners, "Father, forgive them."(Lk.23:34) Agapé is Christian love that extends even to those we've never met and will never meet.

Of course the question comes up, if I am to love my neighbor, who is my neighbor? In Luke's Gospel, that exact question arises. After Jesus affirms the need to love your neighbor as yourself, a lawyer presses Jesus further, asking "And who is my neighbor?"(Luke 10:29) Jesus responds with the parable of the Good Samaritan, designed to teach us that our neighbor is <u>the one who helps us</u>, the one who reaches to us with Agapé love, not, as we might naturally assume, the one WE help.

And yet, when we ask, "who is our neighbor" we sometimes also ask, "are we to love even the unlovable?" In the parable of the Good Samaritan, the person helping the man who had fallen among thieves, was the most unlikeable character of his culture and day, impure and heretical. Though the priest and the Levite are the unlovable ones in the <u>story</u> of the Good Samaritan since they were the ones who passed by the hurting man, the Samaritan was the unlovable one in that <u>culture</u>. In today's world, were the story told again, the unlikeable Samaritan might become someone from another race, another religion or another social strata. But whoever fills that role, if such a person helps us, we suddenly have a new neighbor, whom we must love, as ourselves.

"What shall I do to inherit eternal life?" asked the lawyer. And the answer was, love God and your neighbor as yourself. God spoke to the people of Moses, saying, "Love your neighbor as yourself." And what follows immediately in that passage are the words, "I am the Lord." which is the Divine version of, "Because I said so."

We love our neighbor as ourselves, not only out of self-interest, seeking eternal life, but also out of obedience to the one who still has sufficient authority to say to us, "Because I said so!" We can only hope that our love for God causes us to seek the pleasure of God. And our Creator's pleasure seems tied to the welfare of the world. "For God so loved the world . . ." (John 3:16) Perhaps that's a clue to the full answer to the question, "Who is my neighbor?" The whole world is my neighbor.

There is a companion question to the question "Who is my neighbor?" It goes unstated, and this is it: "To whom will I be a neighbor?" Or, in terms of the parable, "Am I willing to stop to help those in need?" And though we fail often, the answer must be "Yes, I am willing to become a neighbor so that love might grow." In a way, Jesus never answered the lawyer's question. "And who is MY neighbor?" the lawyer asked. Jesus responded by telling a story that offers the implicit answer, "Here is how YOU can become someone else's neighbor. Here is how you can receive love as you become a neighbor." "Who was neighbor to the man?" asked Jesus. And the lawyer replied, "The one who showed mercy." Jesus said, "Go and do the same." Go and become a neighbor so you can be loved.

The version of this commandment found in Leviticus shows us that to love is more than warm fuzzies. We need to scold and to do what our concern for the character and safety of our neighbor demands. Then we love in ways that help us all and we become what God hopes we will become: whole creatures of a loving Creator.

Sometimes, when we think we <u>must</u> love someone; remembering that this is a command, we think that we must, in some way, give in. It's really rather easy to love the Good Samaritan who was supposedly the unlovable one. When you think of it, the Good Samaritan was unlovable only because of cultural prejudice. Remember, he was the GOOD Samaritan. He stopped to help. What about the Bad Samaritans, the ones in our culture, or theirs, who are just bad people, who are unlovable because they are hateful, dangerous and destructive? How are we to love them?

The <u>why</u>, IS easier than the <u>how</u>. We love because we are commanded to love--that's why. But HOW to love is more difficult. Even with the guidance of the great virtues, an awareness of the deadly sins, the Ten Commandments and all the wisdom for living that our faith can give to us, when we've been dealt with shabbily, we sometimes find ourselves asking, "How can I love this person who has wronged me?" The ability to love, which has been given to each of us, is sometimes strained when we seek justice, but the search for justice does not remove the ability to love. Therefore, until we can know justice, love your neighbor as yourselves. That's an order.

THE SIXTH WORD

"You shall not kill."
Exodus 20:13

Mark Twain made the point that all creatures kill, but "Man is the only one who kills for fun; he is the only one that kills in malice, the only one that kills for revenge."[30] This is too true.

On the other hand, Tertullian, in his work, "Apology" written around the year 197 A.D., reminded Christians that ". . . according to our rule of life, it is granted us to be killed rather than to kill."[31]

If we continue to think of the commandments as the ten UTTERANCES of God, or the ten WORDS of God, statements of truth that are evident in a growing relationship with God, among the things that will be evident among us is that in a proper relationship with God, we shall not kill.

"Thou shalt not kill" brings up all sorts of issues. Let me list some of them: murder, war, abortion, capital punishment, drunk driving, self-defense, handguns, assisted suicide. These are tough issues, and the list is not exhaustive. In a way, we're almost eager to deal with these issues.

When Jesus stood before Pilate--this Jesus who had suggested that name calling was as bad or worse than murder (see Matthew 5:21f), who spoke of turning the other cheek-- the crowd, whom Pilate sought to placate, chose to welcome the accused murderer, Barabbas, back into their midst. They could deal with murderers. Too often, it seems, when we deal with issues of life and death, we find ourselves saying, in effect, "give us Barabbas" because we can deal with him and we're uncomfortable with what Jesus demands of us.[32]

The original meaning of the verb, "to kill" which is used in this commandment, dealt with blood vengeance. The point of the law, when understood as a law, was to encourage people not to take the law into their own hands. In the Old Testament Moses set aside three cities of refuge where people, who had killed a neighbor unintentionally and without malice, could go to escape the vengeance that might come upon them because of the death.[33](Deut. 4:41-43) Even so, it was hoped that the people of God would not seek vengeance. Some might, but hopefully not the people of God.

Later, an understanding arose that this word included, not just vengeance killing, but also killing brought about by hatred or malice. That is, this word also meant, murder.

This word of God, then, suggests that the people of God will not take the law into their own hands and kill another human being in an act of vengeance nor will they kill out of hatred or ill will. And the fullness of the word might also include the thought that we will not kill for the sake of expediency.

So what does that mean? It's not hard to make a case against all intentional killing. It's easy to see that murder is wrong. But when we get into questions of war, capital punishment, abortion, suicide, it gets complicated. Then we need to reflect upon our relationship with God. For in a relationship with God, having no other gods before our Creator, we shall not kill. If we claim another God, such as power, wealth, convenience, we might kill. We might kill for good things we put in God's rightful place; things like justice and righteousness that we might idolize. We might kill for those things. But when we do we're taking the law into our own hands.

Unfortunately, our world is not entirely, nor consistently, invested in a relationship with God. We try to make the point that people in a healthy relationship with God will not be involved in killing of any kind, but it's not that simple. Though we believe that God is perfect, we must remember, we are not. Certainly the world is not perfect. And, indeed, our very relationship with God can be nothing but an imperfection, hopefully approaching perfection. The ambiguity in the scripture which allows us to wonder if we should not kill at all or ask if this only applies to murder, may simply be an acknowledgment that in our imperfection, we will, in fact, kill on occasion, be it unintentionally, or supposedly with sufficient justification.

The voice of a frustrated Christianity is asking what Pilate asked, "What shall we do with the King of the Jews?" The Christian heart, hoping for a welcoming response, hears the world shout, "Crucify him!" And, like Pilate, the Christian community asks, what crime has Jesus committed to deserve such brutality? This is the one who brought healing and comfort, assurance and peace, teaching of love to God and to one another. Where is the crime in that?

"But they shouted all the louder, 'Crucify him!'"

And so, released to us is the murderer, Barabbas. And we, as the world, welcome him, rather than accepting the challenge of Jesus to know life in all its fullness. You can have peace that passes all understanding! And the world says: we'll take Barabbas. We're used to him.

One interesting addition to this whole discussion is to ponder just who this Barabbas is, for his name is a most interesting one. Bar-abbas. Bar, in the Hebrew, means "son of". For example, Jesus might have been known to some as Jesus Bar-Joseph. One example the Scriptures give to us is Simon Bar-Jona (Matthew 16:17). And Bar-abbas might cause you to remember what Jesus called God. "Abba, Father."(Mark 14:36) "Abba" being an Aramaic word that some suggest translates best as "daddy"; a very affectionate and intimate designation. And so Barabbas is the son of the father.[34] He too is a child of God. Or, and this is part of the challenge of understanding this passage, it could simply mean that no one knew who his father was, and so he was simply someone's son. It has also been suggested that the name could be stretched to be Bar-Rabbas making it possible that this was the son of a rabbi--a product of religious teaching! He could have been anyone.[35]

74

Whichever the case, the crowd asked for Barabbas, the son of the father. And whichever way you look at it, that's what they got. They got Barabbas, the man, the murderer. And they also got the Son of God.

We probably shouldn't pretend that we are going to end killing in our world. We can only choose for ourselves that killing will no longer occur by our hand, and then pray that God will help us over the rough spots, when we really want to do some killing, as when we are confronted with truly evil people; or, (and the waters can get rather muddy here) when we find that we have killed without meaning to.

There are those who wonder what responsibility we bear, as individuals, when our tax dollars go to deadly efforts, or when the food we buy enables companies to deal unjustly in the world, risking lives for the sake of profit. The way the world works is sometimes so complicated, we may be involved in deadly activities without even knowing it.

I imagine that it will have to be God, an act of God, that will end killing. Only in a world that is no longer like the world we know, will the wolf dwell with the lamb.(Is. 11:6) Maybe we can't end killing in the world. Maybe not yet. Maybe we can't end it in the streets of our cities. But we can choose to end it in our own lives. Maybe that is the act of God, allowing us to serve as the leavening agent to transform the world. We can do what people of God must do, which is to seek the relationship with God which will result, one day, in the fact that we shall not kill.

THE DEADLY SIN OF ANGER

"Do not be quick to anger, for anger lodges in the bosom of fools."
Ecclesiastes 7:9

"You have heard that it was said to those of ancient times, 'You shall not murder'; and 'whoever murders shall be liable to judgment.' But I say to you that if you are angry with a brother or sister, you will be liable to judgment; and if you insult a brother or sister, you will be liable to the council; and if you say, 'you fool,' you will be liable to the hell of fire. So when you are offering your gift at the altar, if you remember that your brother or sister has something against you, leave your gift there before the altar and go; first be reconciled to your brother or sister, and then come and offer your gift. Come to terms quickly with your accuser while you are on the way to court with him, or your accuser may hand you over to the judge, and the judge to the guard, and you will be thrown into prison. Truly I tell you, you will never get out until you have paid the last penny."

Matthew 5:21-26

In the above passage, from the Gospel of Matthew, we see Jesus calling anger a punishable offense, with lesser and greater degrees of seriousness. A more literal translation may be useful, so let's look at how the New American Standard Version relates the words of Jesus. First of all, to be angry with another person makes you guilty: "everyone who is angry with his brother shall be guilty before the court" Even before its <u>expression</u>, anger makes us guilty.

To allow the expression of our anger moves us to another level, on to a greater transgression. "whoever shall say to his brother 'Raca' shall be guilty before the supreme court." Raca is an insult meaning 'fool' or 'empty-headed' or 'good for nothing'. And where a local court would have judged the lesser offense, a higher court will judge this greater offense. And then Jesus says "whoever shall say 'you fool' shall be guilty enough to go into the fiery hell." This is a judgment that can only be made by God.

It doesn't seem so great a sin to call someone a fool, in the first place, so why is it a greater sin to say 'you fool' as opposed to saying 'Raca' or empty headed? The answer is found in the Greek. 'Moros' is the word used in this most significant circumstance. And while 'Raca" means 'fool', 'Moros' means '<u>moral</u> fool'. To call someone a fool might humiliate a person, but to call someone a MORAL fool could impair their very ability to function among their peers. It is the kind of designation that could ruin someone's reputation. And to destroy someone out of anger, was not acceptable to Jesus.[36]

People get angry for all kinds of reasons. Anger is in the

normal range of human emotions; a range given to us by the God in whose image we are created. How then, can anger be a sin?

The quick answer is that anger isn't so much a sin as is the way we handle it. Old and New Testaments alike say, be angry, but don't sin, or, do not let the sun go down on your anger. When it comes to anger, we are to resolve it.

How many times have you known someone to disappear from your life, wondering why, only to find out that they were angry with you, but never told you. How often are we angry with someone but don't make the effort to resolve it? Maybe we don't talk about it at all. We think silence is the kinder path, but hearing Jesus, we find that it's the sinful path.

When anger hurts relationships that are life giving, or hurts our relationship with God, then anger becomes deadly. Then we lose everything, as the scripture says, even to the last cent. The words of Jesus warn us against coming to the altar of God when conflicts in our lives remain unresolved. He instructs us to refrain from offering gifts to God until the wounded relationships have been healed, for if we allow ourselves to live in the prison of unresolved anger, we will not get out until we've lost everything.

Solomon Schimmel writes, "We live in a very angry society, with the highest rate of violent crime in the west. Our courts are clogged with the litigation of angry spouses . . . and claimants bitterly suing each other for pain and injury. We have lost the ability to solve differences calmly and amicably."[37] Perhaps we can regain that ability.

When anger is resolved, it becomes a normal part of our life that we have put in its proper place. The words of Jesus tell us how. Simply put, anger is resolved by claiming responsibility for it and consciously acting to resolve it. To leave our offering at the altar and go our way, claiming responsibility to resolve anger. To take what action is necessary to be reconciled, we deny the deadly power of anger. And notice, by the way, anger is not possessive in nature. This is not about resolving <u>our</u> anger or <u>your</u> anger. <u>All</u> anger needs to be resolved.

The kinds of things we get angry about are usually the kinds of things we can't change, such as a broken down car or a detour that has inconvenienced us. Sometimes we get angry about the kinds of things that need not be changed, like the instructions we've received to improve our golf swing, which are valid but which we simply haven't managed to master yet. But whatever the anger, the best path for us is to heed the words of Jesus, claim responsibility for ourselves and work to resolve anger in our lives.

Here's a challenge. Pick something you're angry about or someone you're angry with; or to be more in line with the scriptures, choose someone who is angry with you. Claim responsibility to resolve the anger and reconcile a relationship. Because as Jesus said, if we don't resolve anger, we're the ones who will pay--even to the last cent.

THE SEVENTH WORD

"You shall not commit adultery."
Exodus 20:14

"Let marriage be held in honor by all, and let the marriage bed be kept undefiled; for God will judge fornicators and adulterers."
Hebrews 13:1-6

There is a child's definition of adultery which says, adultery is "The sin of saying you're older than you really are."[38] That's a kinder story than the one of the flustered nanny, who said, when asked about her job, "I serve a household that includes three children, one adult and one adulteress."[39]

In spite of those stories, adultery, at least as far as the word itself is concerned, is not connected to the word "adult". Rather the word "adultery" comes from a word that means to pollute or to defile. And before we go further, let's make a distinction between <u>adultery</u>, which violates the marriage vow by seeking a sexual partner other than the spouse, and <u>fornication</u>, which violates no marriage vow, but makes no use of it either. That is, those who fornicate pursue sex without being involved in a commitment of marriage.

The next chapter on the Deadly Sin of Lust will speak to most of the issues of fornication, so let's set that topic aside and look more specifically at adultery. To do that, we need to speak of marriage, for marriage is what adultery pollutes.

A phrase little used these days is the phrase: "the sanctity of marriage". It is an important phrase. That phrase draws together two things that should not be separated: marriage and holiness.

Marriage in this culture is too often separated from holiness. When that happens, marriage becomes more a matter of contract and less a matter of covenant.

We have, in our society, a great many weddings, but fewer and fewer couples being wedded into the covenant of marriage.

Contracts are tools of civil order, tools of the state. In the Christian understanding, marriage is more than simply a social or civil contract, it is a covenant.

In the Biblical understanding, covenants are initiated by God and are more than promises made by two people. Covenants of marriage confess an awareness that God has invited two people into a relationship. Covenants are sometimes violated--often in ways that call for our sympathy--and, just as there are consequences in the breaking of a contract, when a covenant is broken, there are consequences too. And though couples often split up over adultery, God is not so hasty to part ways with those who have entered into a covenant. God has an enduring faith in us. Indeed, if two people chose to break a covenant it is an act, not simply of disagreement, it is an act of unfaithfulness. We can be glad that God is more forgiving than we tend to be.

I bring this up about unfaithfulness because it speaks in remarkable ways to this issue of adultery. Among the several definitions of the word, unfaithful, are these:

"1. Not adhering to a pledge or contract; disloyal.

2. Not true or constant to a sexual partner, esp. guilty of adultery.

3. Not justly representing or reflecting the original; inaccurate."

And this one truly caught my eye,

"4. OBSOLETE. Without or deficient in religious faith; unbelieving."[40]

Notice that this usage is obsolete! So now, in terms of the language, is it obsolete to consider ourselves unfaithful in our religion? This is significant! I'd like to think this means that the word "unfaithful" has fallen into obsolescence because everyone is faithful. But I'm not completely stupid. The frightening thought is that, in the case of religious faith, the word, unfaithful, is obsolete because faith is no longer a matter of relevance to the culture.

Newsweek magazine reported on a growing number of young people who are deciding to abstain from sexual relationships.[41] That's something to celebrate, but think about unfaithfulness in religion being an obsolete idea, and consider this: There was a chart in the article listing the "Reasons to wait"[to have sex]. Nine reasons were given, among which were these:

- "Want to wait until I'm in a committed relationship" 87% of the young respondents said they accepted this as a reason to wait. Admirable. People respect themselves enough to not be used.

- "Worry about AIDS" 83% claimed this reason. Understandable. People value their lives.

- "Worry about pregnancy" 84% put a check mark by this reason. Sensible. Bringing another life into the world is serious business.

   And then, this reason:

- "Against my religion." 40%.

No wonder being unfaithful in terms of the faith is an obsolete concept! Eight reasons in the above mentioned survey focused on the person, their fears and desires and the reasons given topped the list with 3/4 or more accepting them as valid. Only one reason focused on a relationship with God and a mere 40% claimed it as personally valid. The message is, "I am relevant, God is not."

Emmet Fox reminds us that in the Bible there is a word

84

that is often used interchangeably with the word, "adultery". It is the word "idolatry".[42] When Jesus spoke to the Pharisees and said "This evil and adulterous generation asks for a sign." He could just have easily said, "This evil and <u>idolatrous</u> generation." Again and again, we return to the place where we see that sin involves losing sight of God and worshipping a lesser God, most often the God of self.

Adultery is morally wrong. It does violence to relationships and to a society. It is wrong, and it is wrong because of the God it worships--the self; and because of the people it forgets--the others in our covenant relationships, whom we might call our neighbors.

In recognizing and honoring a covenant relationship with God, one that teaches us to love God and our neighbor, we will be faithful to God, and to others, with whom we are in this special relationship. Then this particular Word of God will be evident. We will know marriage vows made in love, kept in faith, lived in hope and eternally made new. We will know the sanctity of marriage, and we shall not commit adultery.

THE DEADLY SIN OF LUST

"It happened, late one afternoon, when David rose from his couch and was walking about on the roof of the king's house, that he saw from the roof a woman bathing; the woman was very beautiful. David sent someone to inquire about the woman. It was reported, 'This is Bathsheba daughter of Eliam, the wife of Uriah the Hittite.' So David sent messengers to get her, and she came to him, and he lay with her. . . The woman conceived and she sent and told David, 'I am pregnant.'"
II Samuel 11:2-4a,5

"But I say to you that everyone who looks at a woman with lust has already committed adultery with her in his heart."
Matthew 5:28

Lust is a very old companion to us. Of all the deadly sins, it is the one people are most familiar with, while being the deadly sin we least want to speak of. In Jewish folklore, Lust is considered the oldest feminine presence in all of creation. According to Talmudic legend, a character known as Lilith, was created simultaneously with Adam even before Eve was known. Because she would not serve Adam, say the old tales, she was expelled from the Garden. In the stories she became the mother of all evil and the symbol of Lust.[43]

Lust is that overpowering desire for pleasure, most often associated with sexual pleasure. Like the other deadly sins, lust is so similar to a healthy urge, (we could even say a Godly urge) for love and companionship, and also nearly identical to the natural desire (and certainly a Godly desire) to perpetuate the species, that we might wonder why this is deadly at all. But it is.

We are a society that is struggling when it comes to how we deal with being sexual creatures. Voices trying to present a decent facade, speak of abstinence, faithfulness and morality. Competing against that effort is an even louder cultural voice that suggests lust is not sinful at all, but rather, normal and to be indulged in with abandon. "Sex sells," we say, somehow oblivious to the fact that such a crude usage of God's gift sends the message that we are put in God's creation to use one another rather than to love one another.

The images of sexuality seen throughout the media, is often obscenely irresponsible, but perhaps no worse than approaches to sexuality that suggest we must be giants of some pseudo-morality, almost asexual, clearly something other than the beings God created us to be.

God created us male and female, not so we would deny our sexual nature, but so we might celebrate it. But also, so we would celebrate our sexual nature with integrity and responsibility, rather than with shame. Shame, when it comes to relations between the sexes, is what makes us focus on the physical act rather than on the vulnerable and fallible people that God put in this world to stand, or lay, beside us.

The sin of lust appears when we begin to believe that our desires are to be met simply because we <u>have</u> those desires. Then we fall into the trap, all over again, of considering only ourselves, and neither God nor our neighbor.

The AIDS threat may, or may not, have slowed the permissiveness of our society, but for a good long time, our society has been more than happy to indulge itself. So why would sexually related crimes, from rape to prostitution to child pornography, be on the rise? Wouldn't it make sense to think that if animal desires were being met in this anything goes society, the need to take, or buy, what we want would diminish? It hasn't worked that way. Rather, because we have decided that permissiveness is the way, since we've concluded that it's all right to indulge ourselves, respect for one another has diminished. Reported sexual crimes in recent years have increased at a rate significant enough to suggest that the other people in our lives are no longer neighbors or children of God in our common family, but simply opportunities for us to be satisfied.

This is the deadly sin of lust, which like the other deadly sins, tempts us to make idols of ourselves, to turn what is holy into what is profane. God gave us different sexes, with an attraction that excites us and motivates us, but when that God-given fact is twisted to the point where we can say, "I have physical needs!" ignoring the equally important truth, "I have responsibilities," then things begin to fall apart.

The story of David and Bathsheba relates to us just a few of the dimensions of deadliness that can come to us when

Lust takes control in our lives. Not only does a momentary urge become our golden rule, "Do unto others what will satisfy me," but lust also has the potential to bring about great tragedy. David's liaison with Bathsheba resulted in her becoming pregnant. Because of the lust he felt, David engaged in a great deceit and a great plot; Bathsheba lost her husband because of it; Uriah, Bathsheba's innocent husband lost his life as David sent him to fight in the front lines; and ultimately, the child Bathsheba bore to David died. Lust is deadly indeed.

Remember, a deadly sin is a foundational sin, able to generate other sins. Lust can cause the most excruciating pain. It gives rise to lying, plotting and even murder. The newspapers have shown us that this story of David and Bathsheba is replayed in our day among those moved by lust who have persuaded others to murder the innocent. Sometimes Bible stories are more timely than we, at first, realize.

So, without question, lust is a deadly sin to be avoided, even as we acknowledge that it is nearly unavoidable. In making us creatures with desires, God gave us a great gift even while giving us a great danger. So we must accept that danger, and trust, as Paul wrote, that God "will not let you be tempted beyond what you can bear." (I Cor. 10:13)

Do you remember the interview that raised so much controversy when Jimmy Carter was running for President in 1976? Read the oft-remembered quote in its entirety, as the full quotation has something valuable for us. He said, with admirable honesty, "I have looked on a lot of women with lust. I've committed adultery in my heart many times."

That's what people remember, but what came next was the important part: "God recognizes I will do this and forgives me."[44]

To remember that God knows our foibles and is a forgiving God is important for us. It's important, not for the sake of license or self-justification, but rather for the assurance that though lust is perhaps the most natural sin for us to encounter, God's forgiveness does not end and love is not denied because of our weakness. We have been shown a higher way, a most excellent way, the way of love. Lust sees only the false god of the self. The way of love shows gratitude to God the Creator and respect to our neighbor. The way of love is truly the most excellent way.

THE EIGHTH WORD

"You shall not steal."
Exodus 20:15

It is rather easy to think about stealing. We can name all sorts of examples of stealing, some more obvious than others: robbery, extortion, tax evasion, swindling, just about anything you can think of that involves taking, from someone else, something that isn't rightly yours. But stealing is more than that.

In the Biblical world, the business of stealing, as it made itself known, was a very serious matter. The protection of property was vital in a world that knew few of the comforts we now know and enjoyed few of the scientific advantages we now enjoy. "In a time which did not know modern medicine, the theft of a garment, put aside during a warmer day, could result not only in the owner's bitter suffering from cold through the night, but actually to complications leading even to death. Or the theft of a meager flock, by which a shepherd eked out a literal hand-to-mouth existence, could easily result in intense suffering from malnutrition for the shepherd and his family, always undernourished at best, if not in the actual loss of one or more members of the family."[45]

So you can see, to protect property was extremely important. And yet, we don't live in that time. Our times, at least for a great many of us, are quite different. We might rightly wonder, is this commandment as important to us now, as it was to them, then? And I would say, yes, it is as important to us, but perhaps for different reasons.

Our sense of injustice, roused when something has been stolen, indeed, our very understanding of stealing, is tied unavoidably to our understanding of ownership. And it is our understanding of ownership that needs to be sharpened if we are going to understand, first, how dangerous stealing is and, second, how we might avoid stealing. Yes, how WE might avoid stealing. This is the real concern.

The question we must address is not, how might we convey the value of this commandment to others so we might avoid being robbed? Rather, we must ask, how can we avoid stealing, and why should we avoid stealing? This is not, primarily, about our rights, but about our responsibility.

The Psalmist makes a most powerful point. "The earth is the Lord's and the fullness thereof" (Psalm 24:1) Everything is God's! As Napier suggests, and as we must surely see, to take what has been given in Divine Trust to another of God's children not only violates that person, it violates God as well! We have no right to do that.

Joy Davidman writes, ". . . property is neither sin nor

inalienable right, but a loan, a trust from God."[46] Suddenly, our idea of stealing needs redefinition.

If all we enjoy is on loan from God, what does that say about ownership? How can someone steal something from us if we don't own it? If that's the way things are, why even offer the commandment, you shall not steal? It's impossible to steal, no matter how hard you try! And, wait a minute, if we can't steal, why are there penalties for stealing. The answer is this: what we've been given, God expects us to deal with responsibly. If we steal what God has given to someone else, we are not being responsible. (There are exceptions, by the way. You might remember Jean Valjean in <u>Les Misérables</u>, who steals to feed the family in his care. More on that later.)

Many students of the Bible have suggested this responsibility extends to other commandments.

God gives life. If we take that we are stealing. You shall not kill.

God gives us our relationships. If we undermine another's relationships we are stealing. You shall not commit adultery.

God has granted the capacity to offer worship and praise. If we put a price on that so that some cannot afford to share in devotion, we are stealing. "My house is to be a house of prayer, but you have turned it into a den of robbers."

There are yet other ways to steal.

If there are those who have a need we can meet, that means we've been given an opportunity. If we rob ourselves of the opportunity to meet another's need, we have stolen from ourselves as well as from them. Where there was once a rich opportunity, a cherished possibility, now all that remains is a door closed to those on both sides. Those who should be inside have been robbed of that, and those who should reach out have been robbed too. This is where Jean Valjean, in Victor Hugo's <u>Les Misérables</u>, found himself. Locked door ahead of him, he sought a way in, a window of thievery that he knew he must enter if he was to stop some other circumstance from stealing hope and possibility from the lives of his sister's children.

While we must not steal out of greed, neither should we abide those people or factors which would steal the lives of others by denying them life's necessities. That's one reason why Christians have long been involved in challenging injustice and suffering.

Our greatest blessing comes in understanding that our world is not our world, but God's world, in which we enjoy life and a free will and devotion, only because God has placed the world and all it can offer into our care for a little while. It is a liberating perspective, to be free of property, while free to praise God for blessings. It is a rare person, though, who can follow that very narrow path. And yet the path awaits us, if we will choose to follow it.

If you would seek to live well, in terms of this commandment, don't focus on the issue of stealing, but on the relationship with God. For if that relationship is whole and healthy, we shall not steal.

THE DEADLY SIN OF GREED

"Someone in the crowd said to him, 'Teacher, tell my brother to divide the family inheritance with me.' But he said to him, 'Friend, who set me to be a judge or arbitrator over you?' And he said to them, 'Take care! Be on your guard against all kinds of greed; for one's life does not consist in the abundance of possessions.' Then he told them a parable: 'The land of a rich man produced abundantly. And he thought to himself, 'what should I do, for I have no place to store my crops?' Then he said, 'I will do this: I will pull down my barns and build larger ones, and there I will store all my grain and my good. And I will say to my soul, 'Soul, you have ample goods laid up for many years; relax, eat, drink, be merry.' But God said to him, 'You fool! This very night your life is being demanded of you. And the things you have prepared, whose will they be?' So it is with those who store up treasures for themselves but are not rich toward God."

Luke 12:13-21

Greed is the hunger for worldly things that supplants our hunger for heavenly things. It is an important topic, for

97

greed is the root cause of a sick society, or as the Apostle Paul put it, "the love of money is the root of all evil." And I hasten to add, notice that Paul doesn't say <u>money</u> is the root of all evil, but the <u>love</u> of money. And of course, I should hasten to add as well, that to defend money so quickly might suggest that my <u>love</u> of money is too great.

I've found myself wondering if greed is natural. The child who grabs a toy and says, "Mine!" while placing themselves at the center of the universe is certainly doing something natural. But as natural as that is, I like to think it's also natural for us to see beyond ourselves as we grow up and understand the universality of need among us.

One thing I find intriguingly human about this parable is not so much the issue of greed itself, but the result of greed we can so readily see. We see the result of greed in this passage even before Jesus offers the parable. Jesus was teaching a very large group of people at this point in his ministry. He had grown in reputation, the Scribes and the Pharisees were feeling insecure enough that they were plotting against Jesus, and Jesus now taught his disciples about great spiritual things, including, "the very hairs of your head are all numbered." (Luke 12:7) Because of greed, one man didn't hear a word about what is truly important in life, came forward, interested only in his own gain, and said, "Teacher, tell my brother to divide the family inheritance with me" (v.13) Though it was not uncommon for people to take disputes to their rabbis, I can just imagine the frustration of Jesus. When we try to say something important and someone else's agenda causes them to completely ignore us, it can be maddening.

Jesus responds both in anger and by re-stating his point. In anger he says, Who made me your judge? Then, appealing to reason, he says, Isn't life more than things? Then he tells the parable.

Life is more than things. The people who gather in churches to worship God have already acknowledged that. But so many in our world have not. To see that, you only have to look as far as T-shirts that say, "life is a game and whoever has the most toys at the end, wins". Paul was well aware that life was more than things when he told Timothy ". . . the love of money is a root of all sorts of evil, and some by longing for it have wandered away from the faith." (I Timothy 6:10) Paul understood the warning of Jesus, "Beware, and be on your guard against every form of greed;" (v.15) And there do seem to be many kinds of greed.

We think first of money when we think of greed, perhaps because of what Paul wrote. But there are other kinds of greed. Greed for affection, greed for possessions, (which should probably be subcategorized into such things as clothes, cars, toys, businesses, homes and so on). There is greed for power, for knowledge, for attention.

In the parable, the rich man was truly rich. He was favored by wealth and the land he owned was productive. As he considers his holdings, he has a conversation, not with God in prayer, nor with others who might benefit from what he could offer, not even with family members who probably shared in his wealth. No, the rich man has the conversation with himself, and makes plans to retire in luxury. But, of course, God has different plans.

The point of the parable seems to be, not only that life is

more than things, but also that the price we pay for focusing on ourselves rather than upon God is a high price indeed. Again, as in other deadly sins it is idolatry of the self--putting ourselves at the center of attention, which causes us to lose sight of God and others. In the process we render any work we do, or plans we make, ineffective.

Perhaps you saw the motion picture, "Wall Street". Remembering the words of Jesus, "Beware and be on your guard against every form of greed."(v.15) I watched a speech delivered by the character Gordon Gekko, played in the movie by Michael Douglas. In the speech he says this. "Greed is good, greed is right, greed works . . ." He goes on to say "Greed in all of its forms, greed for life, for money, for love, knowledge, has marked the upward surge of mankind. And greed . . . will . . . save . . . the USA."[47]

When we see the greed of looters and robbers that the news can bring into our living rooms with such graphic immediacy, when we perceive the greed of everyone from rock stars to sports figures to politicians to religious leaders and on and on, we have to wonder, is it truly an upward surge that greed has brought to us? And if greed is so pervasive, why do so many people have no idea what greed is, or how deadly it can be, and worse, have no inkling that what greed generates is sinful?

We should make the distinction between reaping the fruits of our labors with grateful hearts and clutching at profits out of greed alone. There is such a thing as the necessary exercise of power or authority. There is such a thing as real need for affection or knowledge and so on. It is only when we imagine that we must <u>have</u> more, so we can <u>be</u>

more, that greed takes over. William Barclay makes the point that the things for which we are greedy are like sea-water, the more we drink of them, the thirstier we get.[48] When we seek to have more, thinking we will be more, we lose sight of our only appropriate goal--loving God and one another.

In conversations with many church people, I've expressed the thought that while it is every Christian's experience to be born again, and by that I mean coming into the awareness that there is a spiritual life as well as a physical one, it is also every Christian's responsibility to "grow up" again. It seems the height of spiritual adolescence to close our eyes in glee as we discover the personal joy of the inner life and then never open them again to discover the family of God that awaits us both in need and in celebration. For if we don't open our eyes to that, if we don't grow up again in the faith, greed even for God's love can turn us away from God so that we look only to ourselves. "So is the man who lays up treasure for himself, and is not rich toward God." (v.21)

And so I repeat a simple warning. "Beware, and be on your guard against every form of greed; for not even when one has an abundance does his life consist of his possessions."

THE VIRTUE OF TEMPERANCE

"So, whether you eat or drink, or whatever you do, do everything for the glory of God.
I Corinthians 10:31

"So I commend enjoyment, for there is nothing better for people under the sun than to eat, and drink, and enjoy themselves, for this will go with them in their toil through the days of life that God gives them under the sun."
Ecclesiastes 8:15

"To eat, drink and be merry" is how the most familiar version of that passage from Ecclesiastes reads. That's advice I'm willing to take. I need to be reminded, though, as I do those things I enjoy, that the writer of those words was the same writer who said there's a time for everything, and also a time to refrain from most of it.[49]

In an earlier chapter we discussed the virtue of Prudence, which we re-named, "common sense". Now we look at

Temperance, which might be re-named, "moderation". Temperance, is the virtue that helps us maintain a life that wisely observes moderation in all things.

At least since the time of the Christian Women's Temperance Union and its most famous advocate, Carry Nation, temperance has been thought of as applying to the consumption of alcoholic beverages. That wasn't always the case. C.S. Lewis writes of an earlier time when "Temperance referred not specially to drink, but to all pleasure; and it meant not abstaining, but going the right length and no further."[50]

Let me continue with the words of C.S. Lewis because he affirms an important point that the apostle Paul made, that all things are permissible, just not always constructive.[51] Lewis says, "An individual Christian may see fit to give up all sorts of things for special reasons-- marriage, or meat, or beer or the cinema; but the moment he starts saying the things are bad in themselves, or looking down his nose at other people who do use them, he has taken the wrong turning."[52]

All things are permissible but not everything is constructive.

The important part of temperance is to understand how far we can properly go as we indulge in a whole world of pleasures. And it may be that Paul gives us the key to determining that distance. "Do not seek your own advantage, but that of the other." (vs. 24) It is in our service to others that we gain the objectivity necessary to see how deeply we personally can indulge in a pleasure before the virtue of temperance kicks in and says to us: if we have another drink we'll hurt those we love, or maybe kill someone we don't know; if we gamble any more, we'll set a bad example for our children; if we spend another hour in front of the television, our relationships with our families will suffer; if I work more overtime, my spouse will be hurt; and so on.

That spirit of service; of seeking the good of others, trusting God to work for our good in the meantime, is critical to the person who wants to know the virtue of temperance. The positive dimension of temperance says: enjoy God's blessings but never forget to do what serves others. Living life is not just about what serves me.

There is a subtle appetite we humans know that desperately needs the virtue of temperance. It is the hunger to live up to other's expectations. Remember, temperance includes a concern for doing what serves others. It becomes especially difficult to believe that we've gone too far with an appetite when we think we're doing it for someone else. We want to think we'll reach further for those we love. But sometimes we try to live up to other's expectations, thinking it's for someone else, when in fact, it's for the benefit of ourselves, so we can indulge in feeling good about ourselves.

We try to live up to the expectations of others, be they friends, family, places of work or television commercials, so we will be liked, so we will be accepted, so we will be fashionable. We speak of people who work themselves into a heart attack, trying to live up to some expectation of production; or people who grow up with deep anger toward their parents, because, for so long, they lived to please them. The same can go for a spouse. One partner might say, "I know you can do better", and the other will think "I'm going to try to live up to your expectations", but is it to serve the other or is it to remove a personal sense of insufficiency?

To strive to meet the expectations that come upon us from the world around us, so WE can gain praise or acceptance, is an indulgence that can kill us. It is an indulgence that may be permissible but it is rarely constructive. To live for the acceptance of others enslaves us to the idea that we are judged only by what we accomplish. We can thank the Puritans for this aberration.

While it may seem odd to think of it, the Puritan work ethic has worked against temperance. The perceived need to achieve and accomplish above all else is difficult to moderate. What was once the belief that work is morally good, has come to mean, in a popular understanding, work is the only moral good. We think results are the only things that matter.

When the work ethic was strongly promoted in the mid 1800's, it was offered as a means to lift people out of poverty. That is a good motive, and the morally good activity of work can be constructive, if we remember that what we seek is not simply our own good, but also the good of others (like our families, our communities, or our society).

It may be true that the honorable attribute of discipline is what has allowed us our accomplishments. But even discipline should know temperance. Sometimes we must engage in play so we might serve others.

Please don't confuse this with laziness or sloth. Sloth is not a virtue. That's a deadly sin that sees only the self. Temperance springs from an appreciation of God's gifts of pleasure while never forgetting what will benefit those around us.

Temperance is part of a higher ethic designed to lift people out of spiritual poverty.

Temperance assists us in remembering that our lives are gifts to share and not candles to burn out. Treat yourselves and your spouses and your children to more time with you. The time they have to eat drink and be merry <u>with you</u> may ultimately be "all that will remain with them to reward their lives with you which God grants them here under the sun." (Ecc. 8:15, my emphasis and paraphrase) Serve one another, in your families, with more than the basic needs of food and shelter. For most of us, the food and shelter we know is adequate for our real and honest needs. Serve one another's emotional needs too. And exercise some moderation as you program your children's lives. Be careful with the expectations you lay on them.

Here's a thought that will muddy the waters: it could be that temperance should be exercised in moderation. Maybe it shouldn't be ALL things in moderation. Perhaps we should not hold back when it comes to things like faith and hope and love. I don't want to encourage religious extremism, but I would hope that our faith would be always wholehearted.

Remember Paul's words, ". . . whether you eat or drink or whatever you do, do everything for the glory of God." (vs.31) The efforts we make to enjoy more pleasures or to gain more material possessions may or may not glorify God. Our work may give us great joy, and that may glorify God. But marriages that break up because of the foolish pursuit of passing worldly possessions or achievements certainly do not glorify God, nor do the children who learn, mistakenly, that life is about productivity rather than about praising God.

Quite to the contrary, life is about love to others and about praise to God. It is in seeking the good of others that we honor our Creator. The virtue of temperance steers us in our efforts, so that our appetites are controlled in such a way that we are enriched as the good of many is realized.

So whether you eat or drink or whatever you do, enjoy the gifts of God. That's why they're there. Eat, drink and be merry. But remember, do it all for the glory of God and in the service of one another. That will help us to know the Virtue of Temperance.

THE NINTH WORD

"You shall not bear false witness against your neighbor."

Exodus 20:16

"You shall not bear false witness against your neighbor" is a commandment spoken in clear legal language, guarding people against the threat of false accusations. Underlying this timely commandment is the understanding that a person's reputation is of great value. It reminds us that we ought not to tell lies about one another.

Probably the most glaring example of bearing false witness that we see on a regular basis is found in the world of politics. Emmet Fox writes that bearing false witness in the realm of politics, if it continues unchecked, can make democracy impossible. If when people run for office, they are "accused of every foul thing, what will happen? Decent, sensitive [people] will not run for public office."[53] And Fox is right. We wonder about it all the time. We hear so many terrible things about the candidates at election time, it makes us feel like Pontius Pilate, asking "What is truth?" There is a difference between criticizing a policy and calling someone a crook. But sadly, we cross that line too easily. We seem to value reputations enough to try to destroy them, but not enough to build them up.

Bearing false witness is serious business. If you bear false witness in court you can go to jail for it. In Roman times, those who gave false evidence, if discovered, would bear the same punishment as those who were convicted on the basis of the testimony.

To tell tales about someone is an affront that goes deeper than hurt feelings. For if a reputation is impinged upon, it can rarely, if ever, be made whole again.

A religious man said he knew of a plot to overthrow the government. He named the conspirators who belonged to a small and already unpopular minority. And people were ready to believe what they heard.

The false accusations brought rise to years of suspicion, a loss of civil rights, and violence. It was in 1678 that this man, named Titus Oates, started the upheaval against what was called the Popish Plot, which caused English Protestants to look at their innocent Catholic neighbors with fear and suspicion.[54]

Does it sound like a familiar story? Put it in the 1950's and plug in the name "communist sympathizer" and it draws closer to home. But what is most powerful about this story, to me, is that some of the suspicion on the part of Protestants toward Catholics continues to this day.

There are people who build themselves up by tearing

others down. We know those sorts of people. It's an error to think that in destroying the reputations of others, our own improves. The anger of Jesus seemed most pointed at those he called, "Hypocrites". In lying about themselves, trying to make themselves seem pillars of virtue, the hypocrites attempted to make others look morally impoverished. But they were the ones who were really bankrupt; their own poverty became evident as they bore false witness against themselves first, even before they bore it against their neighbors.

Lying about ourselves may be the easiest false witness of all. We want to see ourselves in a most favorable light. We have already been shown, though, Jesus will see through it and God will not be fooled. Nor will many others.

What will improve our reputations is truth. Speaking truth and living in the truth to which Jesus bore witness, brings people to the place where they will believe us, trust us and respect us. The example of a life lived in truth will speak more loudly than words others might use in attempts to ruin our reputations.

Joy Davidman gives some wonderful structure to what shape false witnessing can take. She writes, "[Person A] says, 'I saw John kill his wife on the street corner!' [Person B] says, 'I saw John on the street corner!' [Person C] won't say anything at all. Yet all three of them have seen John on the corner - and know that he did not kill his wife. One lies boldly, one tells an evasive half-truth, one keeps cowardly silence; . . . " But none of the three bear witness to the truth.[55]

There is a difference, isn't there, between the facts and

the truth; between telling no lies and bearing witness to the truth. Rumors and gossip, half-truths and silence, often cause suspicion, anger, hatred and suffering that touches everyone involved. That is not our way. That is not the Christian way.

One of the basic understandings of Christian people is that we are in a family of God's children. All those we love are in our family, but so are those people who offend us, and indeed, we are family to those we offend too. Even the people we despise are family, all children of the same God. And if we are to honor our Creator God, as we deal with others, doing "to the least of these my brothers" as we would do to Jesus, we need to bear witness to the truth. We need to be living evidence that we are people of truth. Bearing false witness has no place among us.

Remember, think of the Commandments as statements of fact, saying that IF we are in a growing and healthy relationship with God, these things will become evident. In that glorious and fulfilling relationship with God, we shall not bear false witness against the neighbor whom we love as ourselves. Let's not kid ourselves, though. We're still imperfect beings. But, hopefully, we are imperfect beings with a direction.

We could ask, just how important are our reputations? As Shakespeare's "Richard II" gets under way, Mowbray says to King Richard, "The purest treasure mortal times afford is spotless reputation."[56] In this life a reputation seems important, but we might ask, if we are good and true people in a good and true relationship with God, how important is our reputation? Put in those terms, we might be inclined to say, ultimately, it's not that important. Our reputation could

112

be inconsequential if we see the important thing being not what others think of us, but what God thinks of us. Still, remember these words, "Let your light shine before others, so that they may see your good works and give glory to your Father in heaven." (Mt. 5:16)

To a world that will increasingly, we hope, be in love with God, our reputation is very important. For if we are people of truth, hearing the truth of Jesus, bearing witness to the truth ourselves, then a reputation that speaks of truth is critical. The people of God must have the reputation of being speakers of truth; for bearing witness to the truth may be the greatest good work we can do.

Remember, the most favorable light is always the light of truth. Even if it is the most difficult light to bear.

In a healthy relationship with God, we shall be true. We shall not bear false witness against ourselves, nor against our neighbors. And our reputation will speak of God, so all might see.

THE VIRTUE OF JUSTICE

"If a man is righteous and does what is lawful and right--if he does not eat upon the mountains or lift up his eyes to the idols of the house of Israel, does not defile his neighbor's wife or approach a woman during her menstrual period, does not oppress anyone, but restores to the debtor his pledge, commits no robbery, gives his bread to the hungry and covers the naked with a garment, does not take advance or accrued interest, withholds his hand from iniquity, executes true justice between contending parties, follows my statutes, and is careful to observe my ordinances, acting faithfully--such a one is righteous; he shall surely live says the Lord God."

Ezekiel 18:5-9

Bad people deserve what they get. At least that seems to be the general feeling among people. Sometimes, if we are particularly offended, we also feel that they certainly don't deserve our love! Justice, we think, demands punishment, but not our love! We ask, how can we love our enemies and still respect the idea of justice when God's gifts extend to all equally; when the sun and the rain fall on the unrighteous and the righteous alike? If we are to make sense of these thoughts and questions, some clear thinking about justice is necessary.

Joseph Klausner, in <u>Jesus of Nazareth</u>, calling on the words of Jesus, wrote, "What room is there in the world for justice if we must extend both cheeks to our assailants and give the thief both coat and cloak?"[57](see Mt. 5:38-42) We wonder where to find justice, when we see the way the world works. The writer of Ecclesiastes felt the dilemma strongly, as he wrote of the "righteous men who get what the wicked deserve, and wicked men who get what the righteous deserve." (Eccl. 8:14)

The best response might be what the reformer, Martin Luther wrote: "If God's justice could be recognized as just by human comprehension, it would not be divine."[58]

Justice in our experience, as we deal with our neighbors, can only be an imperfect justice. Maybe that's why it gets confusing.

Justice is one of the four great virtues that help us to live well. Previously, we've considered the moral virtues of prudence and temperance, which we re-named, "common sense" and "moderation". I don't feel a need to re-name <u>all</u> the great virtues, but C.S. Lewis did a nice job of re-naming Justice, so I'll use it. He calls it "Fairness."[59]

Justice, or fairness, in the sense I wish to consider it, includes, "honesty, give and take, truthfulness, keeping promises and all that side of life."[60] Interestingly enough, though we think that these sorts of good habits are self evident practices to be utilized in any reasonable person's life, we don't see them exercised much in the world. Also interesting is the fact that the word "justice" is found only occasionally in the Bible. Justice is mentioned 120 or so times, depending upon which version you're reading--not all that many. And of those occurrences, only 1 in 20, or so, are in the New Testament. That might make someone think Justice is only an Old Testament concept, but it is not foreign to the New Testament.

In the New Testament you find that Joseph, the husband to Mary, was a just man.(Mt.1:19) and that God's ways are just and true (Rev. 15:3). Those aren't insignificant references, but I think the passages of the Bible that teach us most about justice rarely contain the word, 'justice'. More often they tell us of how to play fair with one another.

The scripture passage from Ezekiel, which heads the chapter, speaks to the need for fair play in religion, in our sexual relationships, when we are dealing with personal property, or with the needs of society and, also, in our financial affairs.

Justice, in this understanding, is not a price paid for an injury. It's a way of life. I wonder if courts or juries think they're really executing <u>true</u> justice when they pronounce a verdict or award a price to compensate for an injury of some sort. William McIlvanney, a British novelist, wrote, "Who thinks the Law has anything to do with Justice? It's what we have because we can't have Justice."[61] Justice is a perfection that we, in our imperfection, move toward. In its highest form, law serves as a compass, pointing beyond itself toward that perfection which is of God.

It's relatively easy to look at the acts of others and expect justice, but it gets tough when playing fair means accepting the responsibility for and the consequences of our own actions, particularly when we've acted stupidly. Still, it happens. And, maybe because it does get tough sometimes, some people in our world see no reason to play fair. When we say, "play fair," we'd better be ready with an answer for those who will ask, "Why should I?" The answer must be a compelling one to us, or we can't expect that it will be convincing to anyone else who hears it.

So why should we play fair? So we may live.

Ezekiel speaks the word of God saying, "Suppose there is a righteous man who does what is just and right . . . he will surely live, declares the Sovereign Lord." (18:5,9)

It may be that one of the greatest injustices we commit is the one that has us spending too much time wondering about our eternal fate and too little time participating in it. And if we wish to know life in its fullness and in its richness, it will involve loving God and our neighbor as ourselves, from which will grow our ability to play fair with ourselves, with others, with the structures of society, and with God. Justice is something we can offer to the world in the way we act, and true justice is born from love.

The Bible does a pretty good job of making it clear that God desires us to live. Hear the last words of the 18th chapter of Ezekiel:

". . . get yourselves a new heart and a new spirit! Why will you die, O house of Israel? For I have no pleasure in the death of anyone, says the Lord God; turn, then, and live."(Ezekiel 18:31b-32)

A rich life, well-lived, is founded in love. If we truly love

God and one another, we tend to do justice. And if we play fair, in honesty and with integrity, faithfully and selflessly, our lives will reflect our participation in eternal life. You just can't live better than that. No amount of unfair gain can match that, and that's reason enough to live with justice as one of our good habits.

THE TENTH WORD

"Neither shall you covet your neighbor's wife. Neither shall you desire your neighbor's house, or field, or male or female slave, or ox, or donkey, or anything that belongs to your neighbor."
Deuteronomy 5:21

The commandment, "You shall not covet" is the tenth commandment, the last in the Biblical list of commandments. As we look at coveting, we should be careful not to confuse coveting with other things.

Though coveting is connected with greed, one of the deadly sins, it shouldn't be equated with greed. Someone I know stated the difference between greed and coveting quite nicely. "Coveting," it was said, "is wanting what belongs to someone else, while greed is just wanting."

Nor should we think that coveting is the same as being envious. To envy what another has is to admire it or even resent it, (presumably because we don't have the same good

121

fortune or possession). Coveting goes a step further by desiring not something similar, but desiring the precise thing that belongs to our neighbor. When we covet, we don't want a house <u>like</u> our neighbor's, we want our neighbor's house. The commandment itself puts it well. Coveting is setting our desire upon what belongs to someone else.

The Apostle Paul wrote to the Romans, "I would not have known what it was to covet if the law had not said, "You shall not covet". But sin, seizing an opportunity in the commandment, produced in me all kinds of covetousness."(Romans 7:7b-8a) This sounds like someone who has known the familiar attraction to that which is forbidden.

What we understand as forbidden to us is most tempting to us. We never seem to grow out of it. And it can lead to coveting if what tempts our desire is something that belongs to our neighbor.

What's the danger? It's certainly not dangerous to the neighbor. The neighbor doesn't have any idea we are coveting what they possess. It could be that stealing will follow upon the heels of coveting, but that's not certain, nor is it the point. Stealing can take place without the object stolen being coveted at all. One might steal for revenge or so that the stolen goods could be sold for money, which is the true and greedy desire. Besides, there's already a commandment against stealing.

The danger in coveting comes in this: when we covet, our life focus shifts, and our desire becomes set upon what another human being has, rather than upon that which God would freely give to us.

There is a difference between aspiring to lofty goals and coveting what belongs to another. Turning our focus from God, where we can truly aspire, risks scattering our energy across a whole world of goals, dreams and desires, that I would contrast against those callings we hear, that vision we gain, the life that grows <u>from</u> God. When we fall into coveting, our priorities become guided by a gaze cast toward an outer horizon that moves us away from God, instead of being guided by a gaze looking to an inner horizon that directs us toward God.

Let me offer you a couple of pithy sayings that might be useful to you as you turn over the idea of coveting in your mind. Lisa Engelhardt has written a little booklet entitled, "Acceptance Therapy". In it you can find these two thoughts. First, "contentment doesn't mean getting all you want, but enjoying what you have." And second, "If you don't like the way your life looks, try changing the way you look at life."[62]

Those two thoughts alone could help steer us away from a life of covetousness. The traps leading into covetousness are not hard to find. From looking at the house across the street or at the car down the block, to nations who look at the various natural resources of their neighbors, if we don't look at the world in such a way that allows us to enjoy and give thanks for what <u>we've</u> been given, we can fall into covetousness.

That might seem trite, but if it was easy to avoid coveting, our world would be a different place. We would be more willing to see, I think, just how fitting it is for someone else to be in possession of what they own.

To covet something that belongs to someone else is evidence that we're missing the point of life. Emmet Fox writes this about coveting: "when you see somebody else in possession of something that you think very nice and very desirable, this is fine. Admire it, but say to yourself, "I am in touch with the Source of that. The lovely house that he has, her happy marriage, his wonderful position, I am in touch with the Source of that."[63] and realize, says Fox, that what belongs to someone else wouldn't fit us even if we did take it.

Remember, when we are in a healthy relationship with God, we shall not covet. The Psalmist understood this.

"Whom have I in heaven but Thee?
And besides Thee, I desire nothing on earth.
My flesh and my heart may fail;
But God is the strength of my heart and my portion forever.
For behold, those who are far from Thee will perish;
Thou hast destroyed all those who are unfaithful to Thee.
But as for me, the nearness of God is my good;
I have made the Lord God, my refuge,
That I may tell of all Thy works."
    (Psalm 73:25-28)

Let your deepest desire in life be set upon growing closer to God and you will begin to see that the way you look at life does not include coveting. Test it. In a vital relationship with God, we shall not covet.

THE DEADLY SIN OF ENVY

"Let us not become conceited, competing against one another, envying one another."
Galatians 5:26

It will serve us well here, to make a distinction between the longing we sometimes feel, when we see someone who is talented or particularly blessed, hoping we will know the same good fortune, but still able to celebrate that other person's joy, over against what is the sin of envy, seen when we resent the good fortune of another.

Thomas Aquinas wrote that envy is ". . . sadness about another's good . . ."[64] When we see someone else's good, and grieve over it, only because their good surpasses our own, then we are falling into envy.

John Locke wrote that, "Envy is uneasiness of the mind," that takes shape when we see the good that has come to another and then feel as though they don't deserve it before we deserve it.[65] And worse, envy is shown when we see bad things befalling another and are not sorrowed by that, but, instead, rejoice in their bad fortune, because it works to our advantage.

You don't have to look far in the Bible for examples of envy. Cain's envy for Abel; the envy of the brothers of Joseph for him; King Saul's envy of David; even the envy among the disciples that made ten of them indignant with two others, when the mother of the two sought for them a place of honor at the side of Jesus.

Even beyond the Bible we see great stories of envy. Perhaps the classic example is "Snow White" in which we see the envy that the Queen feels toward Snow White once her mirror says to her "Queen, thou are lovely still to see, But Snow White will be a thousand times more beautiful than thee."[66]

Typically envy is born when our self-worth is based on competition with others rather than on God's love for us. Envy is an issue of self-image. Envy sets us up in opposition to one another, rather than relating us in common purpose and in common concern with one another.

Envy is not the same as jealousy. Jealousy is that emotion that tries to hold on to what we have, or makes us see, rightly or wrongly, rivals for what we possess. Envy is not jealousy, but jealousy grows from envy. Remember the commandment, "You shall not covet"? Envy may give rise to coveting, but they are not identical. Coveting focuses on some thing, some possession that another person has. Envy focuses on ourselves.

Remember as well, a deadly sin is marked by the many other sins it generates. In The Canterbury Tales, Chaucer names some of those things that grow from envy: backbiting, impatience with God, grumbling, bitterness of heart, discord, accusation and malignity.[67]

In "Snow White" as the Brother's Grimm tell it, we learn that the Queen's envy, "grew every day in her heart stronger and stronger, like a disease, till she had no rest day or night."[68] Eventually the envy led to her desire to kill Snow White.

Often for the innocent, but certainly for the envious themselves, the result of envy is always negative. Abel was murdered and Cain was banished; Joseph was sold into slavery and his brothers were humbled; King Saul went mad, by some accounts, was defeated and died by his own hand; and the disciples were lectured by Jesus, shown clearly their error. Not to raise fairy tales to the place of scripture, but to show there are other examples, even the Queen in "Snow White", to quote the Brothers Grimm, ". . . fell dead on the floor, a sad example of envy and jealousy."[69]

The deadly sins all seem to be tied together because they all grow from the unspoken deadly sin, self-idolatry. The image of God that resides in us, can, if we are so inclined, fool us into thinking that we, ourselves, are the center of the universe. It's then that we fall into these deadly sins, envying as we sorrow at whatever good might befall another that might remove us from the center of attention, taking joy at the misfortune others encounter which might serve to keep us in the throne. To be in that throne at the center of the universe is something we lust for, something for which we are very greedy.

The word "envy" has come into our language by way of

some words which, when loosely translated, can mean "in view." What is "in view" makes the point. In making us the center of attention--of our own attentions--envy directs our attention away from the love of God, away from the giver of worth. It leads us away from the love of ourselves that is appropriate, and what comes into view are others seen now as competitors rather than as brothers and sisters. Envy leads us away from the love we should show toward others. Envy flies in the face of the Great Commandments of Jesus, to love your neighbor as yourself and God with all your heart, soul, strength and mind, because envy teaches: "I am all that's important, even above God and my neighbor."

If you hope to live well, remember that God is God, the giver of worth. Our self-worth is not dependent upon others. It is dependent only upon God. God loves us. That simple truth gives us our worth. That is all. When we feel envy, we need to change our view, to stand with our brothers and sisters, not in opposition to them, for when we stand next to them, what comes into view is the love of God that we all share.

Heed Paul's words, "If we live by the Spirit, let us also be guided by the Spirit. Let us not become conceited, competing against one another, envying one another." (Galatians 5:25-26)

If we return to the place where what is "in view" is the love of God, envy will not be a problem.

THE VIRTUE OF FORTITUDE

"By your endurance you will gain your souls."
Luke 21:19

There's a supposedly true story that comes from the early days of the sport of Boxing. A son won a fight in Australia and sent a telegram to his father, here in the United States, informing him of the news. It read: "Won easily . . . in 84 rounds."[70]

That's Fortitude.

The moral virtues we've discussed previously are not unrelated to this one. They are inter-related, all bringing something beneficial to one another. They contribute to the way we live our lives, for they speak of how we humans might live well in response to God's gifts. Let me give you a brief summary of the virtues we've addressed so far.

The first virtue we looked at was Prudence, the moral virtue that upholds all the other moral virtues. We renamed it "common sense". Temperance was the next virtue we

129

considered. It took on the name, "moderation". It's the virtue that helps us use our common sense to set limits on excessive behavior that can harm us and others. Justice, or "fair play" was next. We made a distinction between justice as legal judgment and justice as a way of living that reaches to all areas of our lives. We spoke of the moral character of individuals rather than the tools of a society. In that way, Justice was seen as an admirable habit rather than as a desired end.

Now we look at the virtue of Fortitude. Unlike Temperance, which seeks to set limits, Fortitude is the virtue which seeks to push the limits, enabling us and equipping us to go just a bit further as we seek to live our lives. C.S. Lewis wrote that the modern English word that comes closest to the meaning of fortitude is "guts". And he added, "You will notice, of course, that you cannot practice any of the other virtues very long without bringing this one into play."[71] And it's true. If we hope to live well in a world that is too often void of common sense, fair play and moderation, it takes some guts.

I've wondered if fortitude isn't a virtue because of all the examples to the contrary that you find in the scriptures. In the Bible you'll find a lot of disobedience, revolt, denying, running away, stumbling and that sort of thing. From Adam, to Jonah, to the disciples who couldn't stay awake an hour while Jesus prayed in the Garden of Gethsemene, to each of us, strength is necessary if we are to live in a way that honors the gift of life. And with all the blunderers in the Bible, you might think that scriptural examples of fortitude are rare. But that's not so.

In the great faith chapter, the 11th chapter of the book of
Hebrews, you can find these words: "And what more shall I
say? I do not have time to tell about Gideon, Barak, Samson,
Jephtha, David, Samuel and the prophets, who through faith
conquered kingdoms, administered justice, and gained what
was promised; who shut the mouths of lions, quenched the
fury of the flames, and escaped the edge of the sword; whose
weakness was turned to strength; . . ." And it goes on. Those
who displayed fortitude in their lives of faith have not been
forgotten in the books of the Bible.

Considering fortitude from a Christian perspective leads
us very quickly to the place where we see that fortitude is
necessarily linked to faith. If there is no relationship that calls
us to task; no object of our love whom we seek to please,
fortitude seems to be of no use. For fortitude to have any
real value, there must be a belief that acknowledges some
purpose and some destiny to our lives; a purpose and destiny
toward which we move. Fortitude has value in such a
journey, even in those instances when the journey is not as
honorable as it could be. When we make ourselves the object
of love, saying that we have faith in ourselves alone, wishing
to please ourselves only, entering into a journey of self-
idolatry, fortitude will push us along. Christians, though, look
toward "a better country" (Hebrews 11:16). In a relationship
with God we learn of our purpose and our destiny, and in
that relationship we pray for strength to make the journey.

There are different ways to look at fortitude. The passage
at the head of the chapter is translated in a variety of ways.
I've used, "By your endurance you will gain your souls"
(NRSV) Other versions say, "By standing firm you will save

yourselves." (NIV) and "In your <u>patience</u>, possess ye your souls." (KJV)   The meaning of fortitude includes all these things, as well as ideas such as strength, courage, and tenacity.

In Fortitude is the fullness of meaning that includes both "the strength of walls and strength of heart."[72]   The strength of walls allows us to withstand sieges that are raised by the many trials and temptations of life.   Strength of heart enables us to persevere as we look to a distant goal.

It's self-evident that it takes fortitude to deal with struggle.   But the reverse is also true.   It takes struggle to build fortitude.   I heard a story of a man who was watching a cocoon on a bush in his yard.   He noticed that the end was opening up and there was a butterfly trying to escape.   Trying to be helpful, the man took his knife and carefully cut away at the cocoon.   The butterfly crawled out of the cocoon and, in a short time, died.   Apparently butterflies need the strength they gain from the struggle to emerge from the cocoon. Without the struggle, they can't survive.

It's the same for the moral life.   If there is never any struggle, our moral character is hindered in its development. I guess Mom and Dad were right when they saw us struggling and said, "It builds character."   Struggle imparts to us fortitude, and fortitude enables us to accomplish greater things and endure greater trials.

As Jesus made his journey to the Cross, through rejection, mockery and scourging, on to a most painful execution, we saw a man of faith, a man who had "guts," who lived well to the very end, withstanding temptation and sorrows, accomplishing what God called him to do.   And in a world where people are too often leaving their moral handholds behind, that journey is our journey. Rejection and mockery, suspicion and anger, even scourging and execution; these all may become a part of our Christian experience.

In Aesop's fable, "The Tortoise and the Hare" we learn the moral, "Slow and steady wins the race." In the slow and steady Christian life, bound in time that moves inexorably forward, we learn that our race is not a race against others, but rather a race in which we hope to become, from the dust of the ground, what God created us to be, jewels that glimmer with the image of God which is set deep within us. It takes fortitude. But it can happen. The book of James encourages us with these words: "My brothers and sisters, whenever you face trials of any kind, consider it nothing but joy, because you know that the testing of your faith produces endurance; and let endurance have its full effect, so that you may be mature and complete, lacking in nothing."(James 1:2-4)

From time to time, people actually do become what they were created to be. It does happen. With Fortitude it can even happen to us.

THE FINAL WORD

"So we have known and believe the love that God has for us. God is love, and those who abide in love abide in God, and God abides in them."

I John 4:16

After looking at the Ten Commandments, the Seven Deadly Sins, the Four Moral Virtues, and the Two Great Commandments of Jesus, it's time to ask the very important question: "So what?" Now that we've made this long journey, what does it all mean? How does all this pondering of the traditional Christian hand-holds of a moral life make a difference?

There is a tale in myth of the ancient king of Corinth, named Sisyphus, who angered Zeus and was condemned to Hades; sentenced to roll a stone to the top of a hill. Unfortunately, once the stone was rolled up the hill, it would roll down the other side and Sisyphus would have to start over again . . . forever.[73]

135

Sometimes, figuring out how to live a good life is like that. We think we have grasped some enduring truth only to have something else turn it upside down. At times it feels like we'll never get anywhere.

At the very least, I hope the preceding chapters have served as a refresher course about the pillars upon which moral life is founded. As people of faith--good, fallible, hopeful, bumbling fools that we are--we can hope we're taking baby steps forward as God's children.

People shake their heads at how crazy our world is, and yet, less than 4 in 10 find their way to a church on any particular Sunday.[74] The Church, it seems, has been losing its authority and its credibility in society. No longer do people accept the Church's voice as authoritative in matters of life. In matters of faith, maybe. The Church is still a credible voice to many people in matters of faith. When it comes to how we should live our lives, though, the Church, for the most part, is granted a certain polite nod, and then generally ignored. And therein lies the problem.

Life and faith should not be separated. Life and faith, when separated from one another become existence and religion. Existence is walking the earth, surviving. Existence allows for no God other than the self. Religion is sitting in the pews, going through the motions for reasons of fear or personal benefit, less and less often for reasons of praising God. And religion has, all too often, made a god of itself as well. But life and faith, have no other Gods but God.

LIFE IS KNOWING THE LOVE OF GOD. That's life in its fullness. What emerges as we come to know God is the knowledge of who we truly are: children of God, whom God loves.

FAITH IS SHARING THE LOVE OF GOD. Belief is not the same. Belief is accepting an idea, beliefs are a list of ideas. Faith is a way of being fully human. What comes forth as we are faithful, sharing the love of God, is an unquestionable credibility, made unquestionable by the simple integrity which marks the honest sharing of love.

And yet, while this is rather straightforward, this is not easy. If it was easy, Oh God, wouldn't it be a world! Knowing the love of God and sharing the love of God, puts us in a place where we unwaveringly follow the Two Great Commandments of Jesus. With life and faith married in our walk through these years that God gives to us, the Ten Commandments, those ten words or utterances of God, are made evident. But it's not easy.

I hear people, on occasion, suggesting that love makes no demands, that love is too easy, too sentimental. But I believe the greatest demand of all is the demand of love.

"Faith, hope and love remain," wrote Paul, "but the greatest of these is love." Faith is difficult. People struggle with it all the time. Hope is nearly impossible, especially in a world that makes us want to despair. But Love is the greatest and most demanding, most challenging, most frightening of all, for love removes us from the center. God is love. God must be in the center of life. But because we want that spot at the center for ourselves, the love that reflects God's image in us, is tremendously difficult. It is not, however, impossible.

The message of God's love that we hope to share with

the world will be authoritative, only as we come to know God. And I don't mean that we gain a voice of authority by knowing ABOUT God, but by KNOWING GOD: by being God's people, by seeking God's wisdom and ways, by resting gratefully in the life God grants and by learning about the image of God that is in us. And the message of that life-in-love-with-God will have credibility only as we risk sharing it. This has always been the great challenge for Christian people. Love is a demanding master. But love also bestows the only meaningful blessings in life.

Jesus knew the way of authority and credibility. The path upon which Jesus walks shows a way of life characterized by common sense, moderation, fair play, and guts, the four Moral Virtues as we re-named them. And with those virtues, we can love God and our neighbor as ourselves, and the Ten Commandments of God will be seen in our lives. The Deadly Sins that all appeared when we placed ourselves at the center of life, will disappear as God returns to the center. And Jesus knew this all. For nearly 2000 years, his voice has been heard as authoritative and credible. For with Jesus, God was at the center of everything. So it must be with us.

Jesus never said, "Be correct." He said, "Follow me."

[1] Lloyd R. Bailey, The Pentateuch (Nashville: Abingdon, 1981) 152.

[2] P.Kyle McCarter, Jr., "Exodus", Harper's Bible Commentary ed. James L. Mays(San Francisco: Harper & Row, 1988) 148.

[3] Ernest Fremont Tittle, The Gospel According to Luke (New York: Harper & Brothers, 1951) 114.

[4] Tittle 114.

[5] Karl Menninger, Whatever Became of Sin? (New York: Hawthorn Books, 1973) 74.

[6] C.S. Lewis, Mere Christianity (New York: Macmillan, 1977) 94.

[7] The Cloud of Unknowing (Garden City, NY: Image Books, 1973) 62.

[8] Lewis 96.

[9] Emmet Fox, The Ten Commandments (New York: Harper & Row, 1953) 67.

[10] www.amazon.com, February 19, 2003.

[11] The Concise Oxford Dictionary of Current English, ed. J.B. Sykes. (Oxford: Clarendon, 1979) "feast".

[12] B. Davie Napier, Exodus (Atlanta: John Knox Press, 1978) 80.

[13] Dr. John Holbert "Exodus" class lecture, Perkins School of Theology. Dallas, 3 Nov. 1982.

[14] Fox 47.

[15] Fox 52.

[16] Fox 48ff.

[17] Frederick Buechner, Wishful Thinking: A Theological ABC (New York: Harper & Row, 1973) 89f.

[18] From a conversation with the Rev. Jim Stein.

[19] Lewis 60.

[20] Thomas Aquinas, *Summa Theologiae* book II, part 1, question 61, article 2, response to objection 1.

[21] Lewis 60.

[22] source unknown

[23] Ralph Waldo Emerson, Lectures and Biographical Sketches(Boston: Houghton, Mifflin & Co.,1883)117.

[24] Robert Raynolds, <u>The Sinner of Saint Ambrose</u> (New York: The Bobbs Merrill Co.,Inc., 1952) 307.

[25] Brevard S. Childs, <u>The Book of Exodus</u> (Philadelphia: Westminster, 1975) 418.

[26] Napier 83.

[27] Childs 419.

[28] Joy Davidman, <u>Smoke on the Mountain</u> (Philadelphia: Westminster, 1954) 61.

[29] <u>The Complete Brothers Grimm Fairy Tales</u>. (New York: Avenel, 1981) 284.

[30] *<u>The Concise Columbia Dictionary of Quotations</u>,* (Columbia University Press, 1990), Microsoft Bookshelf 1992, s.v. "Killing: All creatures kill — there seems to ..."

[31] Tertullian, <u>Apology,</u> in "The Fathers of the Church" vol.10, trans. Sister Emily Joseph Daly (New York: Fathers of the Church, Inc., 1950) 96.

[32] I feel compelled to give credit to the Rev. Dr. John Strassburger who first gave me this useful idea.

[33] Norman K. Gottwald, "The Book of Deuteronomy", <u>The Interpreter's One-Volume Commentary on the Bible</u>, ed. Charles M. Laymon (Nashville: Abingdon, 1971) 113.

[34] I. Howard Marshall, <u>The Gospel of Luke</u> (Grand Rapids, MI: Eerdmans, 1979) 860.

[35] Allan Menzies, <u>The Earliest Gospel</u> (New York: Macmillan and Co., 1901) 274.

[36] William Barclay, <u>The Gospel of Matthew</u>, vol.1,(Philadelphia: Westminster, 1975) 140.

[37] Solomon Schimmel, <u>The Seven Deadly Sins</u> (New York: The Free Press, 1992) 91f.

[38] Dick Van Dyke, <u>Faith, Hope and Hilarity</u> (Garden City, NY: Doubleday, 1970) 151.

[39] <u>The Merriam-Webster New Book of Word Histories</u> (Springfield, MA: Merriam-Webster,Inc. 1991) 4.

[40]*The American Heritage Dictionary,* (Houghton Mifflin, 1987), Microsoft Bookshelf 1992, s.v. "un·faith·ful."

[41] Michele Ingrassia, "Virgin Cool," Newsweek, 17 Oct. 1994:62.

[42] Fox 119f.

[43] "Lilith," Encyclopedia Americana, vol.17 (Danbury, CT: Grolier) 478.

[44] Jimmy Carter. Interview. Playboy, (Chicago: Nov. 1976)

[45] Napier 87.

[46] Davidman 99.

[47] Stone, Oliver, dir. Wall Street. With Michael Douglas, Charlie Sheen. American Entertainment, 1987.

[48] William Barclay, The Gospel of Luke (Philadelphia: Westminster, 1975) 164f.

[49] see Ecclesiastes 3:1-8

[50] Lewis 61.

[51] I Corinthians 10:23

[52] Lewis 62.

[53] Fox 80.

[54] Davidman 106.

[55] Davidman 107f.

[56] Richard II William Shakespeare, Act I, Scene i.

[57] Joseph Klausner, Jesus of Nazareth: His Life, Times, and Teaching, trans. Herbert Danby (New York: MacMillan, 1929)394.

[58] Martin Luther, in The World Treasury of Religious Quotations, ed. Ralph L. Woods (New York: Garland, 1966)522.

[59] Lewis 62.

[60] Lewis 62.

[61] The Concise Columbia Dictionary of Quotations, (Columbia University Press, 1990), Microsoft Bookshelf 1992, s.v. "The Law: Who thinks the Law has anything ..."

[62] Lisa Engelhardt, Acceptance Therapy (St. Meinrad, IN, Abbey: 1992)

[63] Fox 124.

[64] Aquinas, Summa Theologiae book II, part 1, question 84, article 4.

[65] Source unknown

[66] Grimm's 189.

[67] Geoffrey Chaucer, The Canterbury Tales (Encyclopaedia Britannica, Inc.: Chicago, 1952) 517.

[68] Grimm's 189.

[69] Grimm's 198.

[70] Halford E. Luccock, 365 Windows (New York: Abingdon, 1960) 125.

[71] Lewis 62

[72] My friend, the Rev. Sam Tallent first introduced me to this phrase.

[73] Edith Hamilton, <u>Mythology</u> (New York: Mentor, 1969) 298.

[74] George Gallup, Jr. and David Polling, <u>The Search for America's Faith</u> (Nashville: Abingdon, 1980) appendix D.

Made in the USA
Lexington, KY
20 October 2015